Creating
Consent Culture

of related interest

Talking Consent
16 Workshops on Relationship and Sex Education
for Schools and Other Youth Settings
Thalia Wallis and Pete Wallis
ISBN 978 1 78775 081 4
eISBN 978 1 78775 082 1

What Does Consent Really Mean?
Pete Wallis and Thalia Wallis
Illustrated by Joseph Wilkins
ISBN 978 1 84819 330 7
eISBN 978 0 85701 285 2

Let's Talk Relationships
Activities for Exploring Love, Sex, Friendship and Family with Young People
Vanessa Rogers
ISBN 978 1 84905 136 1
eISBN 978 0 85700 340 9

CREATING CONSENT CULTURE

A Handbook for Educators

Marcia Baczynski
and
Erica Scott

Jessica Kingsley Publishers
London and Philadelphia

First published in Great Britain in 2022 by Jessica Kingsley Publishers
An Hachette Company

1

Copyright © Marcia Baczynski and Erica Scott 2022

Hollaback's 5 Ds of Bystander Intervention are reproduced
with kind permission of Emily May.

Excerpts from *The Guidebook to Indigenous Protocol* are
reproduced with kind permission of Bob Joseph.

Front cover image source: Shutterstock®.

A CIP catalogue record for this title is available from the
British Library and the Library of Congress

ISBN 978 1 83997 102 0
eISBN 978 1 83997 103 7

Printed and bound by CPI Group (UK) Ltd, Croydon, CR0 4YY

Jessica Kingsley Publishers' policy is to use papers that are natural,
renewable and recyclable products and made from wood grown in
sustainable forests. The logging and manufacturing processes are expected
to conform to the environmental regulations of the country of origin.

Jessica Kingsley Publishers
Carmelite House
50 Victoria Embankment
London EC4Y 0DZ

www.jkp.com

In loving memory of our mothers,
Joanie Baczynski, who always had my back,
and
Anna Grace Scott, who worked tirelessly for a better world.

ERICA

I would like to acknowledge that I am an uninvited settler living on the unceded and stolen territory of the Sinixt, an Indigenous nation that was specifically targeted for genocide by the Canadian government, and illegally declared extinct in 1956.

Despite this, the Sinixt continue to live on their territory, stewarding and protecting the land, educating the settler community, and fighting for their sovereign rights.

MARCIA

I want to acknowledge that this book was written on my part on the unceded territories of the Ohlone people in the west and the Muscogee Creek people in the east.

JESSICA KINGSLEY PUBLISHERS

We acknowledge that the land on which we gather are the ancestral lands of the Lenni Lenape people, whose presence and resilience in Pennsylvania continues to this day. We take this opportunity to honor the original caretakers of this land and recognize the histories of land theft, violence, erasure, and oppression that has brought our institution and ourselves here.

Contents

Introduction

Imagine a world where no one fears a violation of their boundaries. A world where everyone feels safe in their bodies and confident in asking for what they want. A world where personal agency and autonomy are honored, and people feel free to express their boundaries, preferences, and needs.

What would *you* feel like, living in such a world?

Can you imagine it?

There is a magic that happens when you know that your boundaries will be respected and your desires won't be laughed at. When it is safe to speak up for what you do and don't want, and when it's okay to change your mind. When saying and hearing no feels like valuable information and not rejection. When your body feels, fundamentally and in your bones, safe.

We know because we've experienced this magic, and we want you to too.

How do you make this magic happen? In a word, consent. Earnestly engaging in consent practices is the secret sauce for making interactions fun, enjoyable, and worth repeating.

"Consent" is practically a buzzword these days, but as consent educators with over 25 years of combined experience, we've witnessed the ripple effects when just one person has an embodied, *felt* sense of their own bodily autonomy.

- When a teenager knows her mom will help her to get out of a questionable situation, she becomes more able to make choices without peer pressure.

- When a young man feels in his body that he doesn't owe

anyone sex, he becomes an adult who prioritizes intimate encounters that are pleasurable and healthy.

- When a young man encourages his boyfriend to take the time he needs, they both build trust and intimacy in their relationship that carries on into relationships afterwards.

- When a young woman confidently advocates for the reproductive healthcare she wants, she is able to plan for motherhood in ways that keep her out of poverty.

- When a parent is encouraging and supportive of their daughter's emotional depth and breadth, she becomes a woman who can feel her own emotions without shame or blame.

- When a child feels confident that the adults around them will support their gender explorations, they are less likely to self-harm or attempt suicide.

- When a married couple realizes that they can ask before kissing or touching, it becomes an opportunity to flirt and get to know each other all over again.

- When an eighth-grader at a new school sees that their peers don't tolerate bullying, they seek out other ways to fit in and belong that serve them for the rest of their life.

- When a middle-aged survivor of child sexual abuse discovers the meaning and validity of his boundaries, he leaves his abusive wife and creates a future for himself that is not driven by fear.

We have seen countless examples of personal and relationship transformation like this. But the ripple effects of respect for bodily autonomy are not just internal. They also spread outward, into the community:

- When a woman stops tolerating touch she doesn't want, it changes the tone of the world around her. She becomes an example to others who have been tolerating touch and a warning to those who feel entitled to other people's bodies.

- When a college freshman steps in to get a drunk girl home safely, it builds safety on campus, not just for the girl who got home, but for others who witnessed it.

- When a student is confident that there is at least one adult who will take their concerns about another adult seriously, then abuse cannot continue to thrive in the darkness.

- When one or two bystanders intervene as someone is being harassed on a train, others join in to stop the harasser.

- When a man in a wheelchair confidently asserts his needs and boundaries, the people near him learn not just how to interact with him, but how to be respectful to others who use wheelchairs.

Each of us deserves an opportunity to experience what this feels like. Each of us can create pockets of safety for exploration and opportunities for ourselves and others to experience a true respect for bodily autonomy. Each of us can help create a world where the values of Consent Culture lead the way.

WHAT GETS IN THE WAY?

Most people think that consent is a simple concept. One person asks for what they want, and another person says yes or no. The truth is, consent is far more complex than that, but also richer and more fulfilling.

Interactions between people—everything from casual greetings to sexual play—involve a complex array of factors that are both societal and unique to each individual. Most people want to love and be loved. We want to feel connected and have intimacy with others. So what gets in the way? Negative aspects of socialization, poor modeling, differing communication styles, systemic inequity, and behavior that arises from past traumatic experiences—these all play a role.

Let's briefly look at each of these:

Socialization. As we grow up, we internalize what we see in the community around us. We learn the norms of "how things are done" even when no one has taught it to us explicitly. Some examples include how loudly to talk, how much space should be between people, how much eye contact is appropriate, how conflicts are to be resolved, or how to greet one another. We learn what values are important to the people around us, like whether patience or efficiency is prioritized, what constitutes success, how to think about authority and leadership, and what to pay attention to. These unspoken "shoulds" that we grow up with may become a challenge when they remain unexamined.

Poor modeling. How many of us grew up in a home where we could witness an example of a truly healthy relationship? Then we read books and watched movies in which certain behaviors are held up as romantic, when in the real world those same behaviors could earn someone a restraining order for stalking or harassment. Many young people are getting a sexual miseducation from mainstream pornography, which is akin to learning to drive by watching *The Fast and the Furious*.

Communication. We all have different ways of communicating, even when we speak the same language. Some of us are excellent with reading body language while others are not. Some of us are extremely comfortable with words while others find them confusing. The same action or word can mean different things to different people, due to cultural or individual experiences. It's important to understand our own preferences, strengths and weaknesses in communicating with others, and be aware that others may be coming from a different perspective.

Trauma. No matter the age group or demographic, there will be individuals with a past history of trauma. Trauma can make our common struggles with boundaries even more difficult. Damaged self-esteem exacerbates already tricky social interactions. Learned defense mechanisms that have been necessary for survival can cause a new set of problems. Triggers cloud clear communication.

Systemic inequity. Race, ethnicity, class, gender, disability, sexual orientation, citizenship status, religion or lack thereof are just some of the many areas where a certain status is structurally valued over others. When systems of governance, education, health, and justice are all permeated with bias against some groups of people, and favor towards others, power differentials large and small are created between individuals. As humans, we learn by trying things and seeing what the consequences are. When the consequences are wildly disparate, it can become impossible for those of us caught in the crosshairs to believe that we can say no, ask for what we want, or learn with ease.

Consent doesn't seem so simple anymore, does it? In fact, now it may feel overwhelming. Do we have to become experts in all these complicated and touchy subjects in order to learn and teach consent?

The good news is we don't. Wherever you are in your process, practicing Consent Culture skills will help you to better navigate these complexities. We can't solve all of these issues tomorrow, but we can use our compassion and Consent Culture tools to build better relationships and prevent future harm.

Fighting an old paradigm can be overwhelming and exhausting. But creating a new culture is fun, inspiring and exciting. This is the beauty of this handbook. The interactive and self-exploratory exercises are fun and illuminating. The insights that people gain from doing them begin conversations that spread throughout their social circles. And each exercise is a simple tool for each of us to begin practicing new skills for creating Consent Culture.

HOW TO GET THERE FROM HERE

So, what is Consent Culture? We address this with an entire chapter, but the short definition is a culture in which interactions are collaborative, and as mutually agreeable as possible. In Consent Culture, people feel in control of their own bodily autonomy and boundaries. They feel free to change those boundaries at any time according to their individual desires and needs. Consent Culture is about having respect and compassion for ourselves and all others.

To get from here to there, we have to unlearn some things, and we need to practice new skills until they come naturally. This is where experiential education comes in. Being in a room where Consent Culture is the norm, even for a few hours, can transform people's perceptions quickly.

In this book, we are focusing on bodily autonomy as the foundation of learning about Consent Culture. Most of our examples will be about exploring the ways a person can interact with their body. As you continue to explore the nuances of consent, you may find many other areas where the lessons of consent are applicable and where respecting the other and finding agreement is a valuable way to proceed. This book is a basic overview of many common areas where Consent Culture can begin to be built.

Since this is an introductory-level book, we are prioritizing verbal consent as a means of making interactions explicit. A truly radical Consent

Culture goes far beyond simple exercises or just words. In our ideal vision of the world, people who are unable to communicate verbally due to physical or intellectual disability, language differences or neurodiversity, would experience respect for their bodily autonomy and participate in expanding the range of non-verbal methods by which mutually agreeable interactions can occur. We hope this book provides a foundation for that.

We are not going to create a "safe" world overnight, but if we can create more safety, fun and ease in our inner circles, we can learn to be brave together as we dismantle this culture of coercion. We can help grow social structures that are based on caring and collaboration, rather than individualism and competition.

Part 1

PREPARING

How to Use this Book

This book is intended as an instructional manual for educators and facilitators on how to lead either all or individual parts of the Consent Culture Intro workshop.

You're in the right place if you are:

- an educator of middle school, high school, or college students

- a workshop facilitator wanting to teach consent

- someone who works in sexual assault prevention

- a person who wants to learn more about consent education.

You're also in the right place if your goals are to:

- teach youth or adults how to have healthier boundaries

- help people have better interactions and relationships

- create healthier family, school, and work environments

- prevent consent violations and assault

- create a kinder, more compassionate world.

The Consent Culture Intro workshop was created by Erica and is based on material from Cuddle Party, a workshop and social event co-created by Marcia Baczynski. It is a fun and interactive three-hour workshop that teaches the basics of creating Consent Culture.

You can also use the exercises individually to teach the basics of Consent Culture. If you would like to become a certified Consent Culture

Intro workshop facilitator, there is information in Appendix 1 on how to get further training.

Your students or workshop participants will gain insight into:

- how to raise their relational intelligence

- how to express healthy boundaries and help others feel comfortable to express their own

- how to notice what they want and ask for it

- how to know their own boundaries and what to do if they are unsure about them

- what to do if they or others change their minds

- skills for navigating consent online

- how to give a meaningful apology

- how to collaborate to have the most mutually agreeable interactions possible.

The skills build on each other from the beginning to the end of the book, so we recommend that you introduce them to your students in the same order as they appear in the book.

These are simple but powerful tools that participants can and do take with them to practice in everyday life. These exercises are intended to be enjoyable and informative for anyone aged ten and up. The content is about bodily autonomy, and any touch is optional, of course.

This material is meant for individuals of all genders. At times, we will refer to male and female socialization, with the understanding that many people have unique experiences that do not always fit into the general narrative. Please understand that we are talking about the dominant culture of male and female socialization as an experience that we all come through in our own unique ways, not a monolithic reality. Gender variance is common, yet we all face narratives of who we are "supposed" to be and how we are "supposed" to act.

While gendered socialization and gender inequity are absolutely factors in consent miscommunication and violation, they are not the only factors. Racism, ableism, ageism, homophobia, transphobia, xenophobia, and more play a role in how we are socialized to behave. The common denominators of power differentials, unhealthy boundaries, low self-esteem, feeling unable to say no, feeling unable to ask for what you want, and poor communication, can be found in all humans. We don't believe in separating participants by gender and teaching them consent differently, although this can be done where necessary for cultural reasons.

As human beings we do not come into any interaction, relationship, or space without our identities. And our identities do not come into any interaction, relationship, or space without power. We will discuss power differentials, including the power that comes from being a facilitator.

A note about the language we've used to talk about race and racism

During the writing of this book we looked at different terms such as BIPOC (Black, Indigenous, and People of Color), POC (People of Color), racialized, and People of the Global Majority, and others. In our research, both personal and online, we found that there is no one term that satisfies everyone, and some are more disliked than others.

We settled on the two terms that seem the least controversial, POC and racialized. We use POC when we are talking about people who have been marginalized in a white supremacist system because of the color of their skin, and we use racialized when we are talking about concepts and behaviors.

When we talk about Black people specifically, we capitalize the word Black as this has become the norm in North America for reasons of reclamation and recognition. Many articles have been written about this.[1]

Most of the chapters in this book begin with personal stories which illuminate the purpose of the exercises to be facilitated in that section, before giving you a guide on how to introduce and lead participants through them.

After each exercise, we provide questions for participants to help cement what they have learned. If you have time, there are optional discussion topics for further exploration.

When we (the authors) are talking to you (the reader) there will be no quotation marks around the paragraphs or sentences. When we are telling you what to say to the participants, it will be within speech bubbles. Appendix 9 is just the workshop with no added information, for ease of use.

Please *do* translate this material into your own authentic voice. The way we, the authors, speak certainly won't be the way to talk to all participants. Feel free to put these lessons into language that your participants can relate to. Adjust the examples to make them more age appropriate, as needed. If necessary, seek advice when you are adapting the workshop to different cultural contexts.

Welcome, and thank you for joining us in creating Consent Culture.

Chapter 1

Our Stories

ERICA

Falling down

Have you ever felt as if you were dying? That's how I felt several years ago, as I lay in bed terrified that I would never be able to work again, and would lose everything that I owned. My thyroid was failing, and my adrenals were exhausted. I had no energy and felt hopeless about trying to get back on my feet.

When I could get up I limped about with a terrible pain in my lower back, dragging my left leg behind me. Sometimes I would have shooting pains up and down my spine and biting pains in my hands and feet. It turned out that I had two autoimmune disorders, one attacking my thyroid, and one attacking my spine and joints. I was on short-term medical leave from my job as a control room operator at the local electrical utility. I could see everything I had worked so hard for—feeling secure in my own home, a nice car, the ability to take my little family on vacation—evaporating before me. I was too tired to care anymore. Death is inevitable anyway, I thought, so why not now?

While I spent several weeks in bed I began to realize things. I didn't really like my home or my car that much. I didn't really love my job. Come to think of it, I actually hated my job! I hadn't taken care of myself or put my own needs or wants into the equation of my life for many years. I didn't really love myself. I had been keeping very busy in order to avoid thinking about any of this.

One night, I took a very strong relaxant. I could feel little popping sensations as my spine expanded and the tension held within it released. I had to face the fact that I had been unconsciously scrunching myself into a defensive position for over 40 years, ever since I was sexually assaulted and strangled as a small child. I had become tough, locked that child in the basement of my mind, and carried on. Now, if I was to survive, I had to let that little girl out of my mental prison and learn to love her.

Through a lot of meditation, yoga, and other forms of self-care, my energy began to return. With the help of medication, I was able to get back on my feet. After many months, I was ready to do something again, but now my priorities had changed. I wanted to do more than just work overtime to pay the bills and care for my family. I needed to do things that made me happy and less stressed, that felt meaningful and gave me a sense of purpose.

Finding Cuddle Party

One day during my recuperation, I was scrolling through Facebook when I stumbled on something called Cuddle Party. What was this? I wanted to go to a Cuddle Party! But the closest one was an eight-hour drive away, and there was no way I could drive that far.

Wait a minute. I saw on the site that I could become a Cuddle Party facilitator! Then I could offer Cuddle Party to the people in my area. It was perfect! I hadn't even been to one yet, but I could tell from the website that I needed this. Not only did I want to have more platonic touch in my life, but Cuddle Party also purported to teach better boundaries in a practical way. An inner voice told me that a lifetime of healing my shattered boundaries had led me to this point. I was ready to learn more, and then teach what I had learned. I booked a weekend course to get started on my training as a facilitator.

The first night of the weekend was a Cuddle Party, which I learned was less of a party and more of a non-sexual touch and communication workshop. It was everything I had hoped for! Marcia Baczynski led us through the welcome circle; the first part of the workshop where we learned the rules. These included rules like, "You never have to touch anyone you don't want to at a Cuddle Party" and, "You must ask and receive a verbal yes before touching anyone" and, "If you're a maybe, say no."

At the end of the welcome circle we all agreed to follow these rules and ask for help if we were having any troubles. The asking began. It felt so wonderful to be able to say no and know that it would be honored. It was so freeing to ask for what I wanted knowing that if the recipient of my request didn't want the same thing as me, they would clearly and politely say no. I had never had an experience that compared to this before. I had been right! I needed this in my life.

Over the course of the next few months I trained to become a Cuddle Party (CP) facilitator and got to know some of the wonderful people who are CP facilitators and trainers. I enjoyed the many conversations we had about the complexities of consent and how to handle situations that come up during the workshops. I felt as if I were learning a new language.

Finally, the day came to facilitate my own Cuddle Party. I laid out the cushions and several brave souls showed up. As I led everyone through the welcome circle exercises and presented the rules, I got a front row seat to their personal transformations. I saw people nodding and shaking their heads with wonder as they had powerful epiphanies about how to interact with others. What a joy to see! And after the workshop they told me things like, "I had no idea that I struggled with that until...", "I feel so much more comfortable to say what I want now...", "I've never had conversations like this before, but I can't for the life of me understand why not...", "It seems so simple, but no one is doing it..." and on and on.

I loved seeing the easy level of comfort, spontaneous friendships, and oxytocin-releasing cuddle puddles that happened during the "party" part of the workshop, but my favorite part was the welcome circle and guiding people through the boundary exercises that caused such powerful internal shifts. I wished everyone could experience this!

But as I moved into my third year of facilitating CP workshops, I realized that only a small minority of people were ready to go to a Cuddle Party. As one friend told me, "I don't care what you say, I *know* I'll be forced to cuddle a stranger!" I realized that the very people who would most benefit from the boundary exercises were the same ones who were most disinclined to show up.

MARCIA
Creating Cuddle Party

I wasn't always a cuddler. In fact, when I told my mother that I had co-founded Cuddle Party, she was quite confused, because as a child, apparently, I couldn't sit still long enough to cuddle.

But in 2004, after my co-creator and I started to offer some workshops about communication and boundaries, this new event unexpectedly took off, with a global series of news articles within six weeks after the first event in our living room.

"Why are New Yorkers cuddling?" everyone wanted to know.

"Is this some sort of 9/11 thing?"

"Is this secretly an orgy?"

"Is it a new wellness thing?"

They got one out of three right. Sort of.

But like I said, I wasn't that much of a cuddler. What I was, was a talker. An explainer. And a sex educator.

It started when I was eight years old, precociously reading *Are You There God? It's Me, Margaret.* I asked my mom what a period was, and after she had explained, the next day, I taught my seven-year-old brother everything I had learned, as my parents eavesdropped to correct any misconceptions.

I didn't grow up in a particularly sex-positive household, but my mom was a nurse who worked with pregnant teenagers (many of whom had also been abused), so she wanted to make sure I had factually correct information and a sense of autonomy over my own body. Despite my family's religious conservatism, I learned from an early age that I could say no to people touching me, and my parents would have my back.

As I came of age in the late 1980s and early 90s, sex definitely seemed terrifying. With AIDS looming and no meds available yet that reliably worked, I got the message that sex equaled death, unless you were very, very careful. Pleasure was not part of the conversation, and misinformation was rampant. I could tell that many of my classmates didn't know what was going on, and in high school, I put my factually correct information to work, as a teen peer HIV educator.

Fast-forward through college, safer-sex campaigns involving

condoms on bananas, a women's studies certificate, a sex educator certificate, and a whole lot of realizing that most women and girls did not have a family who had their backs the way I did.

While I was learning all kinds of things about the myriad ways people come together intimately, and how to teach people to do it more safely, one aspect kept coming back to me over and over again: How do you admit, in that bare moment of vulnerability, that you *want* to use a condom?

I became fascinated with related questions. How do you admit you want to be close to someone? What if what you wanted to do was something different from what the other person wanted? How do you move forward with intimacy when you've had your trust violated? What does it mean to connect with someone based on pleasure rather than conquest? How do you develop the skills to ask for what you want? Or to even *know* what you want? How do you set boundaries when you're not sure how that will be received?

In 2000, I moved to New York City. Four years later, New Yorkers were cuddling. It turned out that I was not the only one fascinated with these questions.

It wasn't a 9/11 thing. (Though that was a question we got from reporters early on.)

It wasn't a secret orgy. (By then, I knew people who were doing that in real life and that's not what I wanted to do.)

And while it actually *was* a wellness thing (and there are a whole lot of well-documented positive effects from non-sexual welcomed touch), it turned out that the communication and boundary skills people were learning at Cuddle Party were at least as important to them as the touch itself.

This little, strangely named workshop, with lab time for non-sexual touch, was giving people a safe and well-structured place to practice communication skills around intimacy, affection, boundaries, and touch.

Cuddle Party provides an opportunity to develop and practice these skills *before* the stakes are high, as they are in sex, and before a panic or a freeze response might set in.

The participants get to practice noticing, naming, and enforcing boundaries when it's "not a big deal." (This is important because how others respond to your boundaries when the issues are small is a big clue about how they will respond when it *is* a big deal.)

Providing people with a space to experience having their boundaries respected is mind-blowing. Once you've experienced it, you can't forget it.

Cuddle Party also makes it safer to explore what you actually want, and then ask for it. The participants can slow down, watch and notice what they *actually* want, rather than tolerating, enduring, or going along with something just because it is already happening.

Participants can find their growth edge and explore at the level they feel comfortable with, knowing that the facilitator will have their back if a mis-step occurs or they need support.

Over the years, Cuddle Party has grown to reach hundreds of thousands of participants around the world. With nearly 200 certified facilitators and events having been held on every continent except Antarctica, we have impacted so many people's lives. From learning how to ask for the kind of affection they want, to learning to stand up for themselves and their boundaries, to finally believing that pleasure, comfort and safety in their bodies are their birthright, thousands of people have expressed gratitude for what Cuddle Party has given them.

ERICA

#MeToo

In the fall of 2017, the #MeToo hashtag and movement exploded into the consciousness of the world. As an adult survivor of child sexual abuse, I had taken my assailant to court, and in the process I had helped to change legislation that extended the statute of limitation for cases like mine. But in the early years of my healing, each time I spoke out I felt shamed and silenced. Many did whisper to me that they had also survived such things, but most were not ready to tell anyone else, let alone go public. I felt isolated, even though I knew myself to be part of a very large minority, at the very least. Then, over a decade after Tarana Burke first used the hashtag #MeToo, the floodgates opened. For me this outpouring of truth was like a balm on my wounds. Finally! We were going to talk about this. We were going to do something about this! I felt a renewed urgency to get the education that I was providing to a select few out to everyone.

I spoke to Marcia about creating a new workshop—one that would take the best of the Cuddle Party exercises and add to it, making something that was all about consent education, without the intimidating possibility of cuddling afterwards. She agreed that it was a good idea, and I got to work developing and testing it. I studied different consent education curricula and took the concepts that were presented as lectures and cautionary tales, turning them into new exercises that were fun rather than frightening. I combined these with the excellent boundary exercises from the Cuddle Party welcome circle, and Consent Culture Intro was born.

MARCIA
The book

I was sitting at my desk in my Mission District apartment in San Francisco on a sunny day when I received an email from Erica proposing that we work together on creating a book based on both of our work. For years, I had been meaning to write a book on the basics of teaching consent and building Consent Culture, but my other projects kept taking priority.

Cuddle Party had matured into an independent entity with a board and trainers. I had expanded my coaching practice into group programs and workshops designed to tackle some of the additional nuanced and complex issues people face in their relationships. During this work, I noticed how much difficulty people had in asking for what they wanted and saying no to what they didn't want, and I realized that these skills were central to building a vibrant consent-based world.

In 2010, I had launched AskingForWhatYouWant.com as an umbrella for my coaching and workshops. I centered this work around valuing wants and needs, building better boundaries and addressing how gendered socialization affects these skills. I loved watching my clients gain confidence and agency in their personal lives and relationships. As we worked to build these skills on the individual level, I was also aware that group work—in the form of workshops and group experiences—continued to be necessary to build a new norm, one where people could work together to build consent-based culture.

So when Erica proposed this book, I welcomed the collaboration. I'm excited to finally be bringing these tools and concepts to a wider audience.

OUR HOPES FOR THIS BOOK

The impact of #MeToo on the collective consciousness has led to new conversations and new laws around preventing sexual harassment and assault. Since 2017, the demand for consent education has spread globally. We hope that this book will help to meet that demand.

With over two decades of combined experience in consent education, we have seen enormous changes, and new insights and practices are constantly emerging. However, even with nuanced developments in our understanding of consent, some basic foundational skills remain necessary. Learning how to ask, how to hear no, how to say no, and how to find common ground will always be relevant.

The laws may change, but regardless of how fast or how well they do, we can always learn how to treat one another with more respect and kindness. It will always be helpful to learn how to navigate ambiguity within ourselves and from the people around us. And understanding the ways that trauma and power dynamics can affect interactions will always be important.

This book covers the basic and most central points of consensual interaction. For those of us working in this rapidly changing field of consent education, one of the certainties is that the conversation is evolving every day. This book is an introduction and an invitation to a shift in consciousness that won't end here. This is a beginning.

And now you are a part of it. Are you ready to change things for the better?

Chapter 2

What Is Consent Culture?

Consent Culture is a common phrase, but what does it mean? Let's break it down.

WHAT IS CONSENT?

One of the most common misconceptions about consent is that it's about getting permission. While permission is a *part* of consent, a permission-based model is limited in that it doesn't create space for more than one person's desire or wanting.

Getting permission often sounds like this:

- Is this okay?

- Can I do this?

- May I do that?

While permission isn't at all bad, it's a limiting model. It assumes that one person Has the Thing and the other person's job is to Get the Thing. Whether that's sex, a job, money, help, love, attention, dinner or something else, this "Gatekeeper" model is about getting something, not creating an experience together.

Permission is a *part* of consent—after all, some situations really do boil down to "May I have a cookie?" But there are a whole range of experiences that are more interesting and satisfying when they are created collaboratively.

In short, a fuller model of consent is an agreement about how we are going to interact or share space together.

It's not about permission, it's about *agreement.*

It's not about getting consent, it's about *creating consent.*

But it's not as complicated as you might think.

CREATING AGREEMENTS

How do you create an agreement? You propose stuff! The other person proposes stuff! Then you go back and forth until you know what the agreement is. Kids do this all the time on the playground, but we seem to have forgotten the skill as adults.

Kid A: Let's play tag! You be It!

Kid B: No, I don't wanna be It!

Kid A: Okay, I'll be It!

And they're off!

This is an example of an agreement where the rules are pretty well understood—it's clear. But if you watch kids, they build elaborate worlds with rules and desires that change constantly and are inscrutable to outsiders. They improvise and they throw stuff out there, they keep talking and they fight, and then they sort it out and they keep going until they're done or bored or it's time for dinner. In other words, it's ongoing, mutual, and specific.

This is consent in action. You can quit anytime you feel like it. You may not have an exact script of what will happen, but check-ins are happening along the way.

There are five key skills at play here:

1. Saying what you want

2. Saying yes

3. Saying no

4. Changing your mind

5. Creating space for other people to do the same.

When you are creating an agreement, you are inviting the other person (or people) in. Sharing your enthusiasm for them and the ideas you each have for a positive experience. Giving room to say yes or no. Allowing both yourself and others to have a voice about what's on the table.

In general, it's a good idea to avoid pushing for a specific experience. Instead, put several fun, pleasurable, and acceptable options out there. Then find out what the most mutually comfortable and fun one is and play with the overlapping interests.

Sometimes you'll be creating agreements about something that is no fun at all, like planning a funeral. Even then, offering a variety of options that are acceptable and as positive as possible will make it a less terrible and more cooperative experience.

If it's a "maybe," it's a "no," especially at first, until more trust is built. Don't let scarcity or fear of not getting what you want drive your interactions. You might be surprised at what other cool experiences might happen when you each put what you want on the table and create agreements together.

As you can see, agreements are much more nuanced than simple permission. A good consent agreement is clear, informed, voluntary, sober, act-and-person specific, ongoing, mutual, and active.

But in no way does it need to be formal or stuffy.

CONSENT IS ABOUT MUCH MORE THAN SEX

Another common misconception about consent is that it is exclusively about sex. While it's true that sex is where many of the scariest non-consensual interactions occur, the opportunity to build Consent Culture starts long before that.

This is because consent permeates every aspect of every interaction between people, not just sexual interactions.

Consent informs every movement in the dance between individual autonomy and relationship with others. What at first glance appears to be a simple matter of yes or no becomes a complex web of unconscious expectations, self-esteem, societal status, unexamined beliefs, systemic manipulation, and more. Consent within a culture has everything to do with inequities, entitlements, and shared values.

Many of us learn as children that those who are smaller and less important don't have to consent to be touched, while larger, higher status people have more bodily autonomy. We learn in school that hierarchy is the way of life, and who has more power than who. In every aspect of life, we learn that displeasing those in positions of authority can have dire consequences. There are power differentials everywhere that set the stage for consent violations, both conscious and unconscious.

This is why we can't take consent out of the context of culture. And why we must shift culture to create an environment for consent to truly flourish.

WHAT IS CULTURE?

Culture is commonly defined as a set of traditions, values, language, and beliefs held in common by a group of people. In essence, a culture can be seen as an understanding between people that this set of behaviors are accepted, and those set of behaviors are not. These understandings are largely communicated from generation to generation, and from individual to individual, in an unconscious, unspoken manner, through role-modeling and storytelling.

There are cultures that align with ethnic groups, cultures that are formed by organizations, and cultures that arise from a commonly held passion. We hear of "gamer culture," "festival culture," and "gun culture," which connote a connection and a set of norms between people who are very involved with certain activities. "Workplace culture" describes the atmosphere that is created by management and employees at any particular worksite. And of course, ethnic groups have their own culture defined outwardly by things like language, food, dress, ritual, art and dance; and inwardly by much more nuanced things such as perspective, sense of humor, and beliefs. Always, in any culture, there is an implicit understanding about what is valued, and a shared knowledge about how to express it.

Whole books can, and have, been written on culture and what it is. Our focus is on shifting the current rape, or coercion, culture towards a Consent Culture. ("Rape culture" is a sociological term that refers to settings where rape is pervasive and activities like victim blaming and slut-shaming are common.[2]) Again, books can, and have, been written about rape culture. This is not one of those books. We are focusing on birthing a new normal. And it is easier than you might think. Fighting rape culture is exhausting and hard, but creating Consent Culture is fun and exhilarating.

THE DOMINANT CULTURE IS A CULTURE OF COERCION

In so many ways, and far beyond sex, we have been taught models of coercion as the primary and most "effective" way to interact with others.

From movies to TV shows, to endless bad reality shows, we are taught that romance looks like a man manipulating or chasing a woman relentlessly until she gives in.

Every day, we are swimming in high-pressure sales and marketing techniques to make us doubt our self-assurance and self-esteem, from old-school advertising to modern-day social media influencers.

In the United States, we revere presidents and founders who were, among their other qualities, also slaveholders and rapists.

We see church leaders and spiritual gurus who promote and enforce submission to institutions, rather than encouraging spiritual growth.[3]

We see talk show "doctors" who bully and berate guests into complying with desired behavior, as though that is a professional way to engage with trauma.

We see priests, police officers, educators, and airline pilots transferred for a "fresh start" when they are caught being violent or harassing.[4]

We sing along to songs for decades without realizing they are about rape, coercion or oppression.[5]

We experience it in our romantic relationships, when expressions of ownership and control are seen as romance and love.[6]

We see it when a white woman threatens to call the police on a Black person who is simply minding their own business.[7]

We experience hierarchy in workplaces where some people get perks or suffer less by helping those on top to keep other people down.

We run into it in our friendships when a domineering friend dictates what everyone else in the group does and the friend dynamic becomes one of "walking on eggshells" to keep that person happy.

We see it when fathers feel they "own" their daughters' virginity, and when parents demand "respect" by threatening their children with a beating.[8]

We learn it as children when we are required to hug or kiss our relatives, even when we don't want to.

We see it when a taller person crowds the physical space of a shorter person.

We run into it when a person with a physical disability is treated as though they cannot be trusted to make basic decisions like what to eat, what to wear, or when to cross the street.[9]

While violence (or the threat of it) is one way that coercion culture is enforced, some far more common coercive techniques are shaming, blaming, and threatening a person's sense of belonging. Another is when someone with power simply just *takes* what they want. Perhaps the most insidious way that coercion culture is enforced, however, is by making us believe that we deserve the consequences of "stepping out of line." This is why coercion culture can be so hard to escape from.

The culture of coercion exists wherever someone feels entitled to access someone else's body for their own purposes, or when they feel entitled to that person's compliance in behavior.

On the extreme end, coercion culture looks cult-like, but there are many other ways it shows up that seem innocuous and "normal."

A culture of coercion minimizes, trivializes, and denies harm, leading those who are subjected to it to doubt themselves. Telling a kid to "just ignore" a bully. Asking what a woman was wearing when she was assaulted, as if that, not the rapist, were to blame. Implying that the problems a Black man has are due to his expressions of Blackness and that his problems would go away if he was just more "respectable."

The truth is, anyone can fall victim to coercion culture, under the right circumstances. The subtext is...if you would just *comply*, you wouldn't have this problem. That, in a nutshell, is coercion.

Victim blaming and expecting victims to take responsibility for perpetrators actions are major aspects of coercion culture.

On one side, the culture of coercion says:

- "Keep pushing, even if you get a No."

- "They didn't say no, so it's fine."

On the other side, it says:

- "Don't rock the boat."

- "Being civil and polite is more important than speaking up when someone is being treated poorly."

Victims are blamed for their assaults:

- "You shouldn't have worn that."

- "You should have ignored him."

- "Why were you on that street?"

- "Why did you make her mad?"

- "He hits you because he loves you."

A culture of coercion hurts everyone in it. But we can create an alternative.

WHAT IS CONSENT CULTURE?

This is the most common Google query about Consent Culture. The recently added Urban Dictionary definition of Consent Culture mentions sex that centers around mutual consent, and an emphasis on bodily autonomy. Another website speaks of valuing the other person enough to let them make their own decisions. When you dig deep, the principles of consent include compassion, respect, autonomy, equality, communication, self-awareness, and more.

Consent Culture can look like many things. Here are some we consider central to the idea: Consent Culture is about people feeling comfortable to say no, or yes, as they choose, *without fear of retaliation*. Consent Culture means that the people around you encourage you to know that your own authentic desires are neither more, nor less, important than the desires of others, and you do the same for them. Consent Culture is built when we respect our children's bodily autonomy, and their right to choose who and when to touch.

To us, an essential component of Consent Culture is the recognition that when it comes to bodily autonomy, we all have the right to change our minds at any time. Internalizing Consent Culture means cultivating an awareness of our wants and dislikes, and learning how to express them. It means unlearning messaging and modeling that have taught us to devalue and distrust ourselves.

Consent Culture includes being aware of how systemic inequity and trauma affect people's ability to form meaningful agreements. In Consent Culture, we ask more questions, and assume less. Consent Culture is a shift towards respectful and caring interactions, no matter who, when, where, and why.

A short definition for Consent Culture is a culture which emphasizes collaboration to create the most mutually beneficial interactions possible.

HOW DO WE CREATE CULTURE?

But how is a culture created? There is a lot of talk currently about workplace culture and how to improve it. In the case of a workplace culture, there is a clear leadership within a limited population which can institute policies in order to shift the beliefs, behaviors, and attitudes of the people who work there. Government policies that are designed to prevent harassment and assault in public spaces have also changed local and national cultures.[10]

Shifting the predominant perspective is a never-ending process. When enough people can see and describe an unspoken tradition aloud, the process of creating a new narrative has begun. And surely this is the nature of cultural evolution: each generation carries luggage packed by the one before, only for their children to unpack it and throw some parts out, and add new imaginations.

But when there is a large cultural movement in the world, how does that happen?

During the COVID-19 pandemic, we learned that culture can change rapidly, dramatically, and globally. Literally within days, people learned a new set of acceptable behaviors, and spontaneously began to monitor each other for compliance, from wearing masks, to much more frequent hand-washing, to maintaining a certain distance while in public. While this wasn't smooth across the board, and there was news coverage of public protest about mask-wearing, overall approval of these new cultural norms was widespread and favorable.[11]

At the time of writing, we still don't know what the long-term influence of the pandemic will be. But because it has largely concerned personal space and maintaining physical boundaries, it has moved some previously unconscious behavior into the global consciousness.

#METOO CULTURE SHIFT

Tarana Burke first used #MeToo on social media in 2006 while she was doing advocacy work for sexual assault survivors.[12] It was meant to be a tool for empathy and solidarity among survivors, giving people the courage to stand up for themselves in systems that are designed to silence and shame sexual assault victims.

One night in October 2017, friends of Tarana Burke began messaging to tell her that the #MeToo hashtag was being shared online and was going viral. Caught up in the case against media mogul Harvey Weinstein, actress Alyssa Milano had tweeted, "If all the women who have been sexually harassed or assaulted wrote 'Me too' as a status, we might give people a sense of the magnitude of the problem," and included the hashtag.

A dam burst. A recent resurgence of misogyny and casual sexual assault had been emboldened by the new American President. Generations of girls had been told that they had rights and were entitled to equality, but then grew into women who were devalued, disbelieved, and not protected. They began to find their voices and feel their power in the first Women's March, a congregation in support of gender equality that brought out people in record numbers the world over.[13] A societal apparatus that had worked to keep victims silent was beginning to fall apart.

ERICA

I remember how I felt as I watched the online sharing grow exponentially and globally. I was just turning 51 and had spent the previous year feeling depressed. I had been feeling that I needed to learn to accept that the progress I had hoped to see in my lifetime was probably not going to happen. But I didn't want to accept it. I didn't know how to. So when #MeToo went viral, I was uplifted; triggered, but hopeful. I immediately felt that something monumental was happening. Even with the inevitable backlash, there would be no shutting Pandora's box. The truth was coming out, people would no longer be silenced, things would change.

At first it was just a sensation of the ground shaking, but soon real changes became apparent. More powerful predators began to fall. Although many of them did not have to face criminal court, they lost their jobs, their powerful positions, and they were socially sanctioned. These first concrete consequences made the culture shift feel more real. High-profile court cases were educating the general public on the myths and realities surrounding sexual assault and how people behave afterwards, illuminating the many reasons that survivors do not come forward. All the social and legal obstacles that prevent victims from pressing charges began to be more closely examined.[14] The changes felt more and more substantial.

Organizations were formed to help victims seek justice, and many men were having conversations they had never had before.[15] Consciousness was being raised, and quickly. As expensive lawsuits against companies and organizations that had previously protected predatory employees multiplied, improvements in workplace culture began.

Within a year, local and national governments all over the world began to bring in legislation designed to prevent sexual harassment in schools and workplaces. In America, some states began to mandate consent education,[16] and yearly training to prevent harassment in civil and corporate workplaces. In Canada, provincial legislation was introduced, and federal Bill C-65 was passed, requiring preventative programs in all schools, and federally regulated workplaces.[17] In India, the national government put new emphasis on a program known as POSH, Prevention of Sexual Harassment, and expanded the definition of sexual assault and harassment.[18]

We think this is a very clear and fresh example of how culture can evolve. It begins with our ability to imagine changing things that we have accepted as normal and acceptable up to this moment. It becomes a conversation, and ideas and opinions are adopted or rejected. There is a backlash. Despite the backlash, the new normal begins to be formalized in behavior and the law.

WHAT ABOUT THE LAW?

While definitions of assault and harassment are important to discuss, since many people are unaware of what they are, the law is really a *minimum* bar of how to behave, and is usually about curtailing *the really bad stuff*. The law is generally not very helpful when it comes to how we ought to behave, imagining how to be better with one another, or planning to build a better world. Consent Culture takes the law into consideration, of course, but it is about building up a more respectful, less coercive, and more generous way of interacting with one another. Most laws about assault and harassment focus on a very small subset of what happens to people's bodies, and very little on how to be good to one another emotionally or morally.

Many survivors feel (and are!) revictimized by a justice system that is designed to uphold the status quo of a racist and misogynist worldview.[19] The anatomy of the justice system, the lack of diverse representation within it, and the focus on punishment rather than prevention and rehabilitation, all work to protect those with more proximity to power and penalize those who have been disenfranchised and marginalized by this same power structure.

We need massive changes in the justice system before it will become an effective tool against sexual violence. In the meantime, many police departments in North America are conducting reviews of past sexual assault reports, which had been deemed "unfounded" at alarming rates.[20] There has also been a movement in recent years to clear atrocious backlogs of untested rape kits.[21]

Some colleges are embracing a restorative justice model that focuses on the healing of victims.[22] It's a start, but there is a long way to go, and we must look beyond the law to fundamentally change the ways we treat one another.

(Please see Appendix 4 for more legal information about sexual assault and harassment, and about restorative and transformative justice.)

SUMMARY

To recap, we've talked about how consent is an ongoing, adaptable agreement, and not just about giving permission. We've discussed how the dominant culture is currently a culture of coercion and what that looks like. We've touched on what culture is and how it can be shifted, or recreated. We have laid out what Consent Culture means to us, and what it could look like. Finally, we've addressed the legalities of consent, and why we need to look beyond the law.

This is all background and theory, and we could go on and on about it, but let's move on to practical steps that we can take in creating Consent Culture!

Chapter 3

Laying the Groundwork

People love to be invited into a vision of how the world could be a better place. Guiding them to discover a new perspective on their own terms, and in the context of their own lived experiences, is an art.

That's where skilled facilitation comes in.

WHAT IS FACILITATION?

The definition of "facilitate" is "to make easy: to bring about." As facilitators, we want to guide the experience towards the participants' own discoveries and insights as we try out new ways of interacting, together.

Facilitation may be a new skill to some. It requires listening in a way that makes people feel seen and heard, the ability to ask effective questions, and a constant curiosity. Facilitating a group can be exciting at times as the only certainty is that the unpredictable will happen.

We've put this book together with the intention of giving people who are already educators and facilitators the ability to study and then lead either all of, or individual parts of, the workshop.

BEFORE THE WORKSHOP

If you intend to facilitate all or most of the workshop, here are some things to do beforehand that will set you up for success.

Get ready

Some of Erica's favorite moments in their life have been doing amateur stand-up comedy and improv theater. But as everyone who loves being on stage knows, it is often nerve-wracking and intimidating. It's a really good idea to have a pre-stage ritual before you do any public speaking. For some people, this can be doing a dance to some inspiring music; for others, it may be some deep breathing or a mindfulness practice. Or some combination of activities. It's good to both build up your energy and feel grounded. You want to be upbeat, and also make participants feel that you are sensitive to their needs and holding a safe container for them to explore within.

During the introduction, you'll be setting the tone of the workshop and your level of comfort will inform the participants' level of comfort. This is meant to be a fun workshop, and we hope you'll have fun and enjoy facilitating it. As you get ready to start your workshop, take a moment to clarify your intentions for this event and note what you want to include in your introduction to help fulfill those intentions.

A reminder: The unexpected will always happen. Things never go exactly as planned, but it becomes easier with practice and you don't ever have to be perfect for the experience to be worthwhile.

No matter how comfortable you become presenting any material, each time you're working live with new people, new scenarios will arise that you haven't dealt with before and you'll need to keep learning. It is best to practice coming to the workshop with a beginner's mind. So, if you are a beginner, that's one less thing you have to worry about!

Be present

Leading this kind of workshop material requires you to be clear, centered, present, and in the moment. Like most people, you may have a lot going on in your life. Make sure you take time before the workshop to do self-care and feel grounded.

Erica finds meditation, cuddling, massage therapy, acupuncture, and exercise to be the most helpful activities to get them into a clear and compassionate state of mind. Marcia prefers reviewing her notes, surveying the room ahead of time, looking at her supplies list, having a full water bottle and being well fed.

For you, it may be screaming along to your favorite metal band, journaling, or going for a long drive.

Being present doesn't necessarily mean being cheerful and it is the opposite of glossing over things that are hard. Acknowledging what's going on, to yourself, or possibly to your assistant or to the group, can be a powerful way to be present. You don't have to go into detail or process it. Simply noting that you are having a rough day, or that the news is challenging for many people, and then taking a moment to be with it can be powerful.

Figure out what you need to feel clear and present for others, and make sure you give yourself some of that before the day of the workshop.

Get an assistant if possible
You don't have to go it alone!

Having someone who can help out makes it easier for you to focus on your participants and the conversation at hand. An assistant can help with many aspects of your workshop.

Before the workshop, an assistant can set up the room, check attendance, and make you feel less stressed, which will, in turn, support your participants in feeling relaxed.

During the workshop, an assistant can help you with the visual demonstrations so that you don't have to use a broom or an imaginary partner. An assistant can also help a struggling participant while you continue to facilitate. If a participant is being disruptive or needs extra help, your assistant can tend to them or find the appropriate help for them while you carry on.

Afterwards, an assistant is also helpful for tidying up, giving you feedback and reflecting on what worked and what you might want to do differently next time. This is all about collaboration, so work with someone whenever you can.

Think about who will be in your room
Depending on where you're leading your workshop, your audience might be a lot like you, or they might be very different from you, or from each other. Factors such as age, race, sexual orientation, (dis)ability, neurodiversity, gender, school (or workplace) power dynamics, poverty, wealth and disparate access to resources, education, and how well you account for these things will affect your ability to connect with your participants. Be mindful of the examples you use and the assumptions you have about what their lives are like. Be especially careful not to marginalize someone who is already an outlier in the group. Find ways to invite their experiences in, and validate them.

As a sex educator, Marcia has to be aware when talking about privacy that not everyone has a home or a room where they can know they won't be disturbed. We can't assume that privacy is something everyone has access to.

A woman with a visual disability came to one of Erica's Cuddle Parties. Her specific needs were for people to give verbal descriptions of who and where they were in the room in relation to her. Once the other participants understood this, they were more than willing to find even more ways to make her feel comfortable in the space.

One of Marcia's Cuddle Party regulars uses a wheelchair. Instead of assuming what he needs, Marcia asks him how best to proceed. It is generally best practice to create an opportunity for the person with a need to share with you exactly what they need, rather than guessing, hoping, or doing a bunch of things "for" them without their consent.

When it comes to consent, there are issues that some people deal with regularly that never, ever cross into other people's lives. Many Black people frequently have their hair and skin touched by non-Black people without their permission. Many pregnant people are treated as though their bellies are a petting zoo. Most people with visible disabilities have experienced being moved or touched by people who don't ask whether or not they need help. These are fairly common places where non-consensual interactions occur. It can be helpful, as a facilitator, to familiarize yourself ahead of time with the kinds of non-consensual interactions your audience may have encountered.

You are also one of the people in the room. Consider your own position of power and potential unconscious bias. It's not a failure for a facilitator not to know something. It *is* a failure to think you know everything or can solve every issue your participants run into. We're all learning, all the time.

Learning about other people's lives and experiences that are different from your own is a good ongoing practice for any facilitator. Becoming more aware of different lived realities will serve you well inside and out the classroom. There are some resources at the end of the book to get you started or to help you continue on your exploration.

Set an intention
Setting an intention is a powerful way to prepare for a positive facilitation experience. Very rarely will everything go as planned. We may get caught in traffic and be flustered when we arrive late. Maybe there

was a communication problem and some people thought that they were coming to a different sort of workshop. The possibilities of encountering the unexpected are limitless!

We all have expectations, all the time. When your expectations are met, for example when the workshop goes smoothly, you don't notice that you have them. But when your expectations are turned upside down, it can feel as if you or someone else did something wrong. From there, it's easy to get into a spiral of blame or shame, and it becomes a lot harder to show up for the people in the room.

Expectations can fail, but intentions are always there for you. Having an intention that you can stick to no matter what comes up gives you a solid foundation. Expectations are an expression of performance and perfectionism, while intentions can center you in self-compassion and acceptance. Expectations may be conscious or unconscious and can catch you off guard, but intentions are always something you've thought about and made choices about.

Table 3.1: Examples of expectations versus intentions

Expectation	Intention
That no one will show up.	To create a safe and welcoming environment for everyone who shows up.
That I'm going to be nervous and embarrass myself.	To speak clearly, to lead powerfully, and to choose to be present as best I can in the moment.
That I'll forget what I am saying and look like an idiot.	To be as graceful and present as I can manage regardless of what occurs.
That no one will get anything out of this.	To create the best possible experience for myself and my participants with what is available to me today.
That this experience will amaze everyone who attends.	To allow the attendees to have their genuine reactions to the content, even if it's challenging.
That everyone will have fun and learn something.	To create an environment in which fun and learning are easy to access.
That I will have my notes and materials.	To show up with the tools I have today and provide as good an experience as possible.

When you have a clear intention for what you're doing, then there is room for authenticity and relationship. You'll have more capacity to show up for your participants as they are, and you'll be able to guide them in ways that aren't possible otherwise.

MODELING CONSENT-BASED APPROACHES IN YOUR WORKSHOP

As facilitators and educators, we're taking on two important roles in building Consent Culture.

While we are educating and creating spaces for exploration of what a more consent-based world could look like, we are also ourselves in the process of learning and unlearning what we have been taught about power, coercion, control, and consent.

As facilitators, we have an opportunity to open conversations about things that our participants may not have considered about our larger culture. We also need to expand our own cultural knowledge. All of us have both conscious and unconscious bias due to influences in our lives as we grow up. Some of these are simply harmless shortcomings due to cultural differences, while others are quite harmful because of being raised within systems of oppression. The more we are able to become aware of, and work on, our own biases, the more we can be effective educators.

It is also the case that sometimes we're backed into corners with limited options due to the school or workplace setting we're in, cultural norms, or interpersonal dynamics. Even when we can't change the options available to us or our participants, we can use Consent Culture practices to name the water we are swimming in, or to make our limited choices explicit for our participants.

Here are four areas where you can model a more respectful and inclusive approach in your workshops. You may have additional aspects you want to include in your facilitation to foster a larger awareness of consent. If so, be sure to note them.

1. Land acknowledgement

An important part of creating Consent Culture is acknowledging where consent has been violated. As facilitators, we have an opportunity to model what acknowledging harm can look like.

In North America, the very land we are on was stolen through coercion, violence and the genocide of Indigenous peoples[23] (often referred to as "Native Americans" in the United States and "First Nations" in Canada).

In Canada and in some parts of the United States, the practice of land acknowledgement is becoming more common as a first step towards reconciliation.[24] We encourage people to join this movement towards recognizing the past and present, and creating awareness of what is possible going forward.

Non-indigenous reconciliation with the Indigenous peoples of North America is a hopeful intention to work together in collaboration for a just and sustainable future—"hopeful" because Canada and the US are not consistently taking positive steps towards true reconciliation.

A common misconception (especially in the mainland US) is that the Indigenous peoples who were here are no longer around. While this perspective is starting to shift, it is important to recognize that Indigenous peoples are still here, living on their land, and are neighbors, colleagues, and community members.

Land acknowledgement is one part of that process, shifting our awareness and showing respect for Indigenous peoples and their relationship to the land that all of us are working and living on. It is a recognition of the people whose land you are facilitating on.

As Bob Joseph,[25] author of *The Guidebook to Indigenous Protocol* (www.ictinc.ca/guidebook-to-indigenous-protocol, p.8), says:

> An informed acknowledgement is authentic, accurate, respectful, and spoken with heartfelt sincerity. It is not a platitude. The exercise of doing the research to find out on whose land a meeting or event is taking place is an opportunity to open hearts and minds to the past and make a commitment to contributing to a better future which is the essence of reconciliation.

You may already be in a position to give an informed and heartfelt land acknowledgement, or you may have some homework to do. If so, that's fine! We hope that if you are passionate about creating Consent Culture, you will also be keen to make the connections and do the research in order to be able to add this element of reconciliation to your classroom, or workshop, presentations.

(There are resources to help you with preparing land acknowledgements in Appendix 1.)

2. Using correct pronouns

Part of creating a safe space for everyone is making sure that all genders feel welcome. There is no need to make a speech or give a lecture about why using someone's correct pronouns is important information. Simply offer your own pronouns as a model and offer participants the opportunity to include their own pronouns as part of introducing themselves. Give a short list of examples that they may want to choose from, such as he/him, they/them, she/her, and explain that they are simply stating how a person would like to be referred to by the group.

For example, when Marcia introduces herself, she says, "My name is Marcia. My pronouns are she/her." When Erica introduces herself, she says, "My name is Erica and my pronouns are she/her or they/them."

If participants have more questions on why some people are offering their pronouns to the group, ask them to hold that question until the end of the workshop, or direct them to a website or reading resource. Participants may have both questions and opinions about this. It's a best practice to simply state that having the opportunity to offer our pronouns makes the group a safer place for everyone, and then move on. It is easy to get drawn into a discussion that is not helpful, and possibly toxic, right in the middle of the introductions. Keep things moving.

3. Being trauma-informed

We can guarantee that no matter what group you are facilitating for, there will be participants who are trauma survivors, and so it's important to be aware of how that looks, and how to hold space for those people.

When educators and facilitators are not trauma-informed, they can easily mistake a trauma response for mental instability, or simply bad behavior. For instance, if someone is making jokes because memories are surfacing, or they are realizing that what was done to them was actually abuse, and the facilitator's reaction to their disruptive behavior is very hostile or dismissive, they may shut down emotionally and be fearful of sharing anything.

The first step is being aware that there are people dealing with the effects of trauma everywhere. We are not trauma experts but we will cover some of the basics of being trauma-informed here, and we urge you to learn from the experts and study the subject until you feel comfortable with the fact that you will likely be leading people who are survivors of trauma.

As a facilitator, one of the most important things you can do is to get support around the areas that are emotionally challenging for you. We all have had difficult experiences that have left us with emotional issues to work through. If we haven't worked through our own issues, or found a way to begin expressing and releasing them in a safe place, we'll be very uncomfortable with witnessing others doing this. And we won't be able to be supportive if the emotional challenges of others trigger us, or make us panic. We can only be empathetic, compassionate guides to emotional work once we have personal experience with it and it no longer alarms us.

While studying this subject, we have found it very interesting to learn about post-traumatic growth—the fact that many people grow stronger after experiencing trauma. Although we hear about post-traumatic stress disorder (PTSD) all the time, post-traumatic growth is actually the more common reaction to trauma.[26] On top of that, studies have shown that there are ways to transform PTSD into post-traumatic growth, such as sharing your feelings with empathetic people rather than holding them in, and finding ways to bring meaning to hard experiences by using them to help others.

Whole books have been written on this subject,[27] and you can find resources in Appendix 1. We encourage you to explore this growing body of knowledge.

4. Mandated reporting

A discussion of relationships and consent may cause participants to disclose abuse that has happened to them. It's very important that you are emotionally and logistically prepared for this to happen. You should have a plan with options for participants who present as upset or disassociated, or who disclose abuse.

You could have a counselor on standby, and/or have information available to access counseling. For participants who just need a breather, you could have a designated safe place for them to go. And before you begin, it's important for you to know the mandated reporting requirements for that area, and inform the participants of your obligations.

If you're talking about consent with people under the age of 18 and you are mandated to report disclosures or suspicions of child abuse, you need to let the participants know this at the very beginning of the workshop. Participants need to explicitly understand the consequences if they do decide to disclose. Otherwise they will rightfully feel betrayed if they feel safe enough to share and then discover that you are in turn compelled to share the information with authorities, taking further action completely out of their control.

In some places, all adults are required by law to report child abuse; in other areas, the mandate to report depends on your occupation.[28] You need to be familiar with the rules wherever you are. There are resources on this in Appendix 1.

DURING YOUR WORKSHOP
Participants with questions

In any workshop, questions will (and should!) come up. Some are important to address in the moment, and some might be distractions from the flow of the workshop. Learning to navigate this takes practice, but here are some tips:

- If someone interrupts you with a question, you have the option to set the tone that this is an interactive workshop by taking the time to answer it if it's relevant, and to address their concerns rather than ask them to hold their question.

- If you know that the question will be answered later in the workshop and answering it now could lead into a long tangent, simply tell them that it is a great question and that it will be answered later in the workshop.

- If someone's question is one that is irrelevant to the workshop, offer them resources or offer to discuss it after the workshop is over.

Some people may push back against some of the ideas presented in the workshop. Stating that different genders are socialized differently, that racialized power dynamics exist, or that people have different communication styles may cause "The Explainers" in the group to have a vocal opinion about why this is or isn't true or why it should or shouldn't matter.

Although we want dialogue and interaction, if someone starts explaining the workshop to you or pontificating about why you're wrong about something, it's time to cut them off and keep them from derailing the momentum. This can be done politely but firmly, by saying things like, "That's an interesting idea/opinion/point of view, and I'd love to discuss that further with you after the workshop but right now we have to move on." Or you can offer to discuss it with them during a break.

Both Marcia and Erica have been participants in workshops where one of the other participants absolutely hijacked the entire event because they had a constant need to be heard, and the facilitator didn't know how to handle it. If you have a group member like this, you'll probably start to realize it around the third time they interrupt or have a story to share before anyone else has had a chance to speak. Getting them on track can sound something like this, "I'm really interested in what some of the other participants have to say. Let's hear from someone else," or, "Let's let someone else have a turn now," or, "Some participants need a little encouragement to join the conversation. Let's see if someone else is waiting to share something."

One way to be proactive about these kinds of issues is to start your event with a group agreement, which we'll talk about in the next chapter. If you're concerned about how you'll handle these possible situations, practice by getting friends to interrupt you while you're rehearsing the workshop so that you'll be prepared.

What if things go sideways?

You should have a plan in place in case a participant is triggered by memories, or by another participant. A quiet seat off to the side, an assistant who can step in, or leaning on existing support from the organization or school can help.

Be aware that participants who are being disruptive or reticent may be sending out a call for help. Let your group know whether counseling is available to them if they need to talk to someone in depth or more privately. Point out that helplines are listed in the participant handout.

Sometimes, a participant will say something so dismissive or shocking that it stuns the room. Navigating this is one of the harder things about good facilitation. One option is to pause and have everyone take a breath. You might have the assistant stay with the room while you pull that participant aside (or vice versa). Sometimes the group will need to process what was said together.

It is important to be aware that, in these instances, your own implicit biases might make you inclined to give more empathy or priority to the person (or people) in the room with more power than the person (or people) with less. This is a common response, because we all want to be liked and we all have our own unconscious points of vulnerability, but it can be very harmful to those who are already marginalized.

In a heated moment, it can be easy to fall back on unconscious bias. Marcia learned a great question from author and anti-racism activist

Rachel Cargle for checking herself when there's conflict in the room: "Who am I protecting here?"

Having a clear intention, as mentioned above, will also guide you back to where your focus should be after a disruption.

While participants will sometimes be disruptive due to feelings of discomfort or awkwardness, we have had few really difficult experiences of participants being acutely triggered or breaking down. That's why we recommend being prepared for this possibility rather than being taken by surprise.

AFTERCARE

As facilitators, we often put a lot of work into preparing for an event, but we may not think of what we need afterwards. Marcia has noticed that sometimes she or her colleagues will have a big emotional crash after some workshops, or need help integrating the experience. It's a good idea to think ahead of time about what you might need after your event.

You might need to stretch or lie on the ground. It might help to write in a journal or make some notes about what you want to do differently next time. Some facilitators like to take a hot bath or drink a glass of wine afterwards. Others might find a brisk walk or a conversation about an entirely unrelated topic to be just the thing.

As you gain experience facilitating, you will discover what works best for you. It can be helpful to plan or schedule it in advance, so you know you're getting what you need.

SOME QUESTIONS FOR YOU

Here is a checklist to help you determine if you are ready to facilitate:

- Have you facilitated workshops before?
- If not, have you taught in school?
- Or taken a course on facilitation skills?
- Have you memorized the material, the exercises, and the order of presentation?
- Have you practiced the workshop material with family or friends?

- Have you practiced working with potential disruptions or distractions?

And here are some questions to ask to prepare for the workshop:

- Are you ready to be present and open for your participants? It's important to have a self-care routine to clear your own mental clutter and center yourself.

- Have you figured out the logistics of getting there early, and having everything you need?

- Do you have an assistant?

- Have you set an intention?

- Have you thought through who is likely to be in your room and what additional needs or perspectives they might have?

- Have you decided which discussion questions you would like to focus on?

- Have you copied handouts for your participants?

- Have you researched the land you are facilitating on for a land acknowledgement?

- Do you have a decompression plan for afterwards?

RESOURCES

You'll find a range of resources to help you cultivate your facilitation skills in the appendices.

SUMMARY

Okay, you're ready! To recap, you've memorized and practiced the workshop material, found an assistant if possible, and prepared for potential disruptions. You've decided which discussion questions to ask, and figured out how much time you have for questions and discussion. You've set an intention. You've thought about who will be in the room and prepared a land acknowledgement for your introduction. You've done your pre-workshop self-care and warm-up to get into the right state of mind. You're calm, centered, grounded and present. Let's get started!

Part 2

FACILITATING THE EXERCISES

Chapter 4

Creating the Container

People of all ages are better able to learn and explore when they understand the framework in which they are operating. When the boundaries and expectations of your workshop are clear, it allows participants to focus on the material at hand.

It's important to let participants know what to expect from the beginning, and then stick to the timeline and structure that you have laid out. If you're facilitating the entire workshop, you can let people know when it will end, and when you plan to have bathroom breaks. If you're only sharing some of the exercises from the workshop in a class setting, this same principle applies.

This is what we mean by "creating the container"— creating an intentional space for a specific purpose.

WHAT TO COVER

At a minimum, give your students information about what they are about to embark on, about how long it will take, and what they can expect to happen. This is an important part of creating a safe space. People will trust you more when they see that you stick to the structure you've outlined.

If relevant, this is the time to explain your mandate to report so that participants can have the information they need to understand the consequences of disclosing abuse. (There is more information about this in Chapter 3 and Appendix 1.)

If participants are unfamiliar with the building and need to know where things are, share this information right at the beginning. It's essential to go over emergency exits, and any other safety information.

The introduction only lasts for a few minutes, but is so important. You're introducing yourself, setting the tone and letting participants know that you are steering the ship and they are safe. Be present, look people in the eye, and when they share something personal or ask a question, thank them. When you get them to introduce themselves to the group, acknowledge each person after their introduction by thanking them or welcoming them.

During the introduction, you'll also share information such as what to do if they need support during the workshop, and the fact that they are not required to participate and can simply watch if they are uncomfortable. Remind them that the more they participate, the more they will get out of it.

It is *very* important that participants understand they can sit out any part of the workshop that feels uncomfortable to them. Far too many "consent" workshops railroad the students into mandatory participation, undermining the experience of choice, which is core to Consent Culture. If desired, you can give a question or reflection topic for participants to consider while they sit out.

This is also the time to give a heartfelt land acknowledgement, and a short and simple explanation of how people can introduce themselves with their pronouns.

It creates a more cohesive experience for everyone if you go around the circle and have each person introduce themselves at the beginning, even if you think that they all know each other already. People can be asked what they hope to get from the workshop, or to give one word that describes their current state, or perhaps state the last movie they watched, or some other non-intimate bit of personal information.

GROUP AGREEMENTS

Every step of your container-building process is an opportunity to reinforce the values of consent-based interactions, and group agreements in particular are a fantastic place to model the areas you'll be talking about in the workshop.

Details of these agreements will vary depending on the group size, age, familiarity with one another and so forth, but they might include things like raising hands, listening with curiosity, being willing to clarify what is meant by a word or phrase, sharing from your own experience using "I" statements, making space for people who talk less often, maintaining confidentiality when sharing about what you learned, and no cross-talking.

Be sure to make the group agreements clear and straightforward. Then ask everyone to intentionally and explicitly opt into them by raising their hands. Once hands are up, you may want to encourage them to keep them up a moment longer, so that everyone can look to see that the others are opting in as well. This starts to build a framework of accountability.

If a participant is resistant to opting in, you or your assistant may wish to talk to them separately to find out what is going on for them and what they need, in order to avoid putting them on the spot in front of all of their peers. Resistance can pop up for a lot of reasons, and entering into that conversation with curiosity and patience may help that participant open up to you.

You can learn more about group agreements in Appendix 3.

INTRODUCING YOURSELF

When you introduce yourself say a little bit about why you are the workshop facilitator or how you came to be a consent educator. If you are already the teacher for this group, you could explain why you're leading these exercises. We've given an example here of sharing our vision for the future and inviting people to join us, but you certainly don't need to say something like that if it doesn't work for you or your group. Be authentically you, be present, and you'll be fine. We start something like this:

WORKSHOP EXERCISE

Beginning the workshop

> Hello everyone, and thank you for being here. I have a vision of a future in which we as individuals and societies are kinder, more compassionate and more respectful to others and ourselves. This workshop is one tool to help achieve this vision and I thank you for joining me on this journey!

Take a few minutes and ask people to introduce themselves. Participants can give a name, state their pronouns, and say a little bit about what they hope to get from the workshop. You can also ask people to introduce themselves with one word that describes their current state of mind, or a fun fact about themselves, such as a favorite place, movie, or hobby.

> I would like to begin by acknowledging that we are holding this workshop on the traditional and unceded lands of the Sinixt Nation [for example].
>
> It's important for you all to know that I am required to report any disclosures of abuse. If anyone feels that they cannot stay in the room or needs assistance during the workshop, there is a support plan, and it is this...

If applicable, let the group know about your mandate to report. Please see Chapter 3 and Appendix 1 for more information.

> This is an interactive and experiential workshop, and we're going to be talking about consent, but mostly we are going to do exercises that help us practice what we are learning. If at any time you don't want to participate in an exercise, please feel free to sit on the sides and watch, but I encourage you to participate as much as possible, because the more you participate, the more you will get out of the workshop.
>
> Before we get started, let's make some group agreements about what is and isn't okay behavior in this group. Does anyone want to suggest an agreement that will make them feel safer during this workshop/exercise?

Write down ideas from the group. If the participants don't mention them, ask the group about adding the following:

- Respecting when someone is talking/no cross-talking.

- Having a designated space for sitting out if you're uncomfortable.

- No comments/observations from people while they are sitting out.

- Raising hands to speak.

> Alright, so can we all agree to these guidelines? Great, let's get started.
> Let's talk about consent. Does anyone here have a definition of what consent is?

Encourage a short discussion on what consent is. Be present, listen, and thank people for speaking. If people are hesitant to say anything, joke that it is not a test and there are no right or wrong answers, you're just curious to hear what ideas everyone has on the subject.

> Great! Thanks. In the past few years, the popular concept of consent has evolved really quickly from "No means No" to "Get a verbal Yes" to "Anything but an enthusiastic Yes is a No." Another way to look at consent is as a collaboration, or "How are we going to play together?"
>
> Many people think that consent is simple. One person asks for something and another person says yes or no. But the reality is that there is nothing simple about it. For starters, hopefully more than one person is asking for what they want! And it is likely that compromises are being made. There are a lot of factors that make creating consent between people more complicated. We'll talk about those factors as we go through the exercises.
>
> When we are collaborating to make our interactions as mutually agreeable as possible, that is Consent Culture. We're going to talk more about collaboration and how to do it in a minute but first let's do some boundary exercises.

SUMMARY

And that is the introduction! To recap, we've introduced ourselves and any assistants, and we've led the participants to introduce themselves. We have provided information about the space, where the bathrooms are, when breaks will be, and given a timeline for the workshop. We've created a group agreement about how we will keep each other safe. We've provided an overview of what we are about to do and what is and isn't required of the participants. We have shared our responsibility to report, and shared the safety plan for triggered participants. Finally, we've given a general introduction to the concepts of Consent and Consent Culture. On to the exercises...

Chapter 5

"No" Is a Complete Sentence

ERICA

Have you ever had sex when you didn't want to? I'm not talking about rape. I'm not even talking about compromising with a loving partner when you feel a bit meh about having sex, and they are promising to make it extra fun for you. I'm talking about just deciding to let someone you don't particularly care about or desire have sex with you. When I was younger, I did this many times, and although this may be shocking for some, for many this will sound familiar.

There are a lot of reasons why people (who aren't acting out of fear of violence) will just give in to another's desire and have sex when they don't want to, but essentially it boils down to damaged personal boundaries. We didn't talk about enthusiastic consent when I was a young person, and it was expected that some people would try to push through neutrality and resistance. You can see such behavior presented as romance in scene after scene of the movies of that era, and even now.

That's why I was so surprised when this happened: I was hanging out with a good male friend that I really liked but was not attracted to. He made a move and before I knew what had happened we were kissing. After a minute or so he noticed that I wasn't responding the way he had hoped, and asked me "Do you want to do this?" I paused and told him, "I guess not really." And he answered. "Okay, let's not." I was shocked. This was not what

I was used to. I asked him, "You're okay with that?" And he said something that was such a revelation to me that I've never forgotten it. He said, "Why would I want to have sex with someone who isn't into it?"

I was shocked because my experience up to that point had been that most guys did not care if I was into it, and took anything less than me screaming and running away as a Yes. But how right it felt to hear him say this! Obviously, my friend's response was the right one, and a clear demonstration of care and empathy.

That was the other side of the equation. My side was that when someone who was attracted to me assumed that I was a Yes, I would often just go along with it.

These are the two sides to this consent miscommunication that need to be addressed and there are solutions for both sides. It is my side of the equation that has had less examination. Damaged self-esteem, broken boundaries, toxic socialization to be people-pleasers, and cultural biases about avoiding conflict leave many of us defenseless against deliberate predators or even just obliviously aggressive partners.

There is also the often-misunderstood autonomic response to a perceived threat, the freeze response, which makes it impossible for people to act. This is the most common response during sexual assault, and we will talk about this more in Chapter 11.

In my own life, there were times when I didn't want to hurt the other person's feelings, there were times when it seemed easier than arguing, and there were times when I felt that I owed them sex because they had done something nice for me. Essentially, I believed what the other person wanted was more important than my own personal autonomy.

MARCIA

Something I often work with clients on is noticing how exhausting it is to go along with stuff even when they don't want it. One exercise I'll have a client do is called "Tolerations." It goes like this: Write down at least 50 things you are tolerating in your life, big or small. It could be something in your environment, like a squeaky door or a messy car. It could be something internal, like a habit you want to break or negative self-talk. Or it could be something interpersonal, like a parent who frequently pushes boundaries or a friend who talks over you.

What emerges is a picture of the trade-offs my client has made in her life. Now it is important to realize that everyone—even the most well-adjusted people—makes trade-offs. It's a necessary part of life. But for many of my clients, the interpersonal tolerations in particular are extremely illuminating. A client will frequently have big patterns of pleasing and appeasing at the cost of her own well-being, happiness, safety, security, or pleasure. In exchange for these things, she doesn't have to speak up, "rock the boat," or set boundaries.

For my client, like many of us, it seems like an okay trade-off at the time. "I don't need to risk an unpleasant interaction if I just carry this for a while." She may take pride in how much she can carry, how much she doesn't complain. She may have learned early on in life that making other people happy at her own expense is a good thing, or she mistakes martyrdom for love.

But when "a while" turns from a few hours to a few days to months to forever, and the trade-offs pile up, she frequently finds herself depleted, exhausted, and burnt out. She may discover she is surrounded by people who take her for granted, unable to re-member what makes her happy, or in a job or marriage that leaves her deeply unfulfilled.

All to avoid the discomfort of saying no in a given moment.

When I talk to a client about this kind of people-pleasing, it's usually about much more than simple awkwardness or not wanting to bother others. Frequently there's a deep uncertainty about her right to her own body, feelings, and priorities. It's often unclear to her whether she is asserting her own boundaries or asserting her will over other people, because for much of her life, others have been asserting their will over her.

And almost always, no one has ever taught her how to mean-ingfully say no.

SAYING NO IS A SKILL THAT HAS TO BE LEARNED

We tell these stories to illustrate the absolute importance of learning how to say no, frequently, early, and often. Far too many young people grow into adults, learning how to accommodate others without any regard for their own personal boundaries.

To some degree, this is unavoidable. As our colleague, Betty Martin[29] says, even under the best of circumstances, we all learn how to go along with things happening to our bodies that we don't want, before we learn to speak. We get picked up when we don't want to be, get our diapers changed when we don't want them to be, we get put in our cribs when we want to be running around. In a worst-case scenario, the child's boundaries are never even acknowledged, and terrible abuse occurs. Even if our parents were somehow perfect in supporting us in our boundaries as we get older, these early experiences teach our nervous system to tolerate, endure and go along with things.

Most of us have parents who were somewhere in the middle. We *all* have to actively learn how to say no to things we don't want. We have to learn to counter that early programming to tolerate and go along with things happening to our bodies that we don't want.

This is why building a culture of consent is so important, and why, at every turn, we need to make space for our own and other people's no.

As a facilitator, you have an opportunity to create a space where your participants can openly and fearlessly practice saying no. For some of your students, this may feel terrifying, or revolutionary. Others will be more well-practiced. Making space for an honest no is one of the most powerful ways we can create Consent Culture.

HEARING A NO

That's a lot about saying no. Now what about hearing a No?

In the old Gatekeeper model, discussed in Chapter 2, where one person is asking for permission, and the other says yes or no, a No means one thing: rejection. And rejection, frankly, sucks. Not only that, but we make it mean all kinds of things.

Some people turn it internally: I suck, I'm a loser, I asked for the wrong thing, I never should have asked, no one is ever going to like me, *I should kill myself.*

Other people turn it outwardly: YOU suck, you don't know what you're missing, you're a bitch, you're an asshole, you should kill yourself, *I'm going to kill you.*

Asking for something you want, especially when you want to be close to someone else, is vulnerable and getting a "No" can feel dire. (We'll talk about that more in Chapter 10.) Learning to handle difficult emotions could be an entire workshop on its own. But as a short-cut, it can be helpful to look at underlying attitudes of entitlement.

For the people who turn inwardly against themselves, it's often a problem of a *lack* of entitlement to the things that are properly within their sphere. We all are entitled to want things. We are allowed to ask for them. Our desires, in and of themselves, are not the problem, and shrinking them down shrinks us down as people.

For the people who turn it outwardly, it's a problem of being *overly* entitled. We are *not* entitled to have access to another person's body just because we want it. We are *not* entitled to get our needs and wants met on our own timeline, according to our own preferences and priorities. We do *not* get to just take what we want from other people.

That old Gatekeeper model doesn't give us a lot of room to interpret a No in other ways. If the gatekeeper says no, it's either a problem with you or with them. The awkwardness or discomfort that follows a No almost needs to be channelled into one or the other.

FROM GATEKEEPER TO COLLABORATOR

Consent Culture offers another way to interpret a No.

Because we are two (or however many) people coming together to find an agreement about how we want to play or interact with one another, a No is not necessarily a rejection. Instead, it becomes *information.*

The other person is not rejecting you. Instead, they are telling you where they are at and what they are and aren't available for. Instead of it being a referendum on *who you are as a person* and what *you* are putting on the table, it's about *them.*

Even when we don't feel entitled to someone else's body, it can still be disorienting or challenging to be on the receiving end of a No. We might be worried that now things are going to be awkward. Or we might just straight up not know what to say next.

That's why learning to gracefully receive a No is such a crucial skill. When we take the other person's No as information about them, instead of a gatekeeper's judgment about us, we can navigate our friendships and intimate relationships with more skill and ease.

Imagine that you really must get to a store on Main Street before it closes to get something you need. It's late, and you are walking north as quickly as you can. Knowing that you are cutting it close, you ask someone if Main Street is that way, pointing north. The person tells you, "No, Main Street is actually southeast."

While you might be frustrated, angry, disappointed, or annoyed that you are going in the wrong direction, and that you might not make it in time to the store, most of us don't get angry about the information itself. Even when you're upset, you might say, "Thanks" before heading towards Main Street or giving up.

That's the clue for where to go next when you get a No. When you're relating as a potential collaborator, even if you're disappointed, you can say "Thank you," because the other person is sharing information with you to help you better navigate your world.

The truth is you never know exactly why someone is saying no to you. It *might* be because they aren't into you. Or, they may not be interested in that activity, or they may have a conflict. They might like you but not know how to make a counter-offer. They might have something else going on that has absolutely nothing to do with you. Or they might not be interested in you *right now*.

None of those reasons is meant to be an excuse to be pushy, but rather to look at the No as information.

Receiving a No gracefully can sound a lot of different ways, but starting with a heartfelt "Thank you" is a good thing to practice.

Some other examples include:

- "Thank you for letting me know where you're at."

- "Thank you for that information."

- "Thanks for trusting me enough to say no to me."

- "Thank you for taking care of yourself."

"NO" EXERCISES

These exercises put participants into partners and groups. Please see Appendix 2 for best practices for doing so.

> Okay we're going to do a speaking exercise now. I'll be getting you to talk about touch, but no one is actually going to touch anyone.
>
> I'm going to ask you to get into the pairs that we've formed, and remember who is an A and who is a B. A, your job is to ask B, "Would you give me a hug?" and B, your job is to say, "No." Please say nothing else other than the word "No."

Even though you just instructed people to say only no, expect to hear all kinds of joking and making excuses. There will be laughter.

> Great. Thank you. Now please trade places and do it again. So B, this time you will be asking for the hug, and A, you will say the word "No."

You'll probably have to give people about 30 seconds or so for each of these exercises in order to allow everyone a chance to get all the way through them.

> Great. Thanks for doing that. How many people felt uncomfortable saying no?

As you ask these questions, raise a hand as encouragement to participants to also raise their hands if they agree.

> How many people felt like making saying no into a joke? How many of you really wanted to explain to the other person why you were saying no, even though we all just heard me tell you to say no?

People will be laughing and pointing at each other because they did just do that.

> Most people have a really hard time saying no. We don't want to let people down or disappoint them. We don't like conflict and we don't want to hurt people's feelings. Many people will do a LOT to avoid saying no, even when they really need to.
>   Let's try another exercise.
>   This time A will ask for a hug and B will say no. After B says no, I'd like A to say, "Thank you for taking care of yourself." Do that now please.

Once you feel they have all finished, have them trade places and do it again.

> Awesome. Thanks. Did it feel different saying no that time? What did you notice about how that changed the dynamic? How did it make you feel saying/hearing "Thank you for taking care of yourself"?

Allow for some discussion. Participants usually want to share what they are experiencing.

One of the ways that we create Consent Culture is by making sure our partner knows that we will hear and honor their No. When we actually thank our partner for honestly telling us that they are a No, we can help to undo a lifetime of learning that we are somehow being a bad person if we say no.

Before we go further into hearing and honoring No, I have to say, should you—or they—even be asking? Sometimes there are power differentials that make it almost impossible for people to say no, and in those cases even asking for touch is considered a form of harassment. If someone is your boss, supervisor, teacher, mentor, counselor, or just has a lot more power in the world than you do, they shouldn't even ask to touch you, or suggest that they would like it if you touch them. If there is a large power differential, it is the person with more power who must make sure that non-consensual or inappropriate actions don't happen.

Okay, on to consent in a situation where the people involved are on a relatively equal footing.

For the following demo, you can ask your assistant to join you, or use a broom or other prop.

Does this look like consent?

Lunge-hug either your assistant or a prop while simultaneously asking, "Hey want a hug?" so that you are already in full embrace before you finish asking the question. This should get some laughs.

Another way to create consent is to actually give your partner the time and space to be able to consider the request and give you an answer. If we ask and the person is silent that is also a No. Silence is a No. Anything but an enthusiastic Yes is a No.

Anything but an enthusiastic yes is a no.

If you have an assistant you could do a demo here of a consensual hug with an ask and an enthusiastic Yes. You could also demonstrate thanking the assistant when they say no to a hug.

And by thanking the person for clearly stating their boundaries we can help them to feel more comfortable expressing themselves honestly. A person who has your best interests in mind will want to know what you truly want.

But what if someone says no to you and you are really struggling to accept their No? Maybe it really did hurt your feelings or you were super attached to how you imagined things going if they said yes. Please DO get help with working through your feelings and find someone to talk it out with. Your feelings are valid and it's good to talk about them. But please DO NOT expect the person who just said no to you to be that person. Having to hear about your upset feelings could feel like coercion to them, as if you're trying to guilt them into changing their answer.

OPTIONAL DISCUSSION TOPIC

If you have extra time, and it is appropriate for your group, use the following story to encourage further discussion. This should be appropriate for all age groups.

In January 2017, an English television show called *The Secret Life of 5 Year Olds* aired an episode that focused on gender.[30] Five-year-olds were separated into groups of boys and girls and served lemonade that was very salty. The group of boys immediately spat it out with exclamations like, "This is disgusting!" while the girls sipped the lemonade (or pretended to) and said more polite things such as, "This is very good, but could I have a glass of water?"

Some questions you could ask the group about this story are:

- Why do you suppose the boys and girls have such different reactions towards their teacher who served the lemonade?

- Do the different reactions surprise you? Why or why not?

- If these different kinds of reactions in the face of an unpleasant experience continue on into adulthood, how do you feel that would impact communication between the genders?

SUMMARY

To recap, we've led the participants through a couple of exercises on saying and hearing no and discussed how most people have a hard time with this. We've introduced a tool for honoring when others say no. We've demonstrated what consent does *not* look like, what enthusiastic consent does look like, and touched on power differentials between people and how they affect consent. Finally, we have talked about what to do if you are hurt by someone else's No. Moving on...

Chapter 6

But it's Hard to Say No!

ERICA

I'll never forget when I began to learn about saying no. It was in the hallway of a university dormitory and I was enjoying being with some new friends. My boundaries were pretty much shattered as a child, and although I had an independent spirit, I had internalized that my body was not mine to control.

Some friends and I had just ordered pizza to share and we were hanging out in the hallway goofing around. We were talking about a movie that had just come out, and one of the young men acted out a scene by slapping my face lightly. I just let him, and I noticed his look of surprise. He did it again and once more I just stood there and took it. He started to laugh. He called out to the others, "Look, she doesn't even fight back" and stage-slapped me again. I wondered what all the fuss was about. What was I supposed to do?

Then he turned and tried to do the same thing to one of the other young women. Before his hand got near her face, she countered and blocked his strike! Not only that, but she hit him back!

It was as if a hundred light bulbs went on in my head at once. For some reason, I needed to see that demonstration to understand that this was not only a possible but reasonable response. It had not even been on my radar as a possibility. And being told the same thing verbally would not have had the same effect. *I needed to see it.*

Young people don't need to see a lack of consent modeled. Most of us at any age, have experienced plenty of that, from a variety of angles.

What we all need is to see is a lack of consent labeled and clearly identified as such, along with as many examples as possible of what communicating a clear No can look like.

WHY IS IT SO HARD TO SAY NO?

This work of creating Consent Culture sometimes feels the hardest when it comes to teaching people what to do when they are a No. In the last chapter, we talked about how No is a skill that needs to be learned.

If only that were all we were up against!

There's a phenomenon that happens constantly: an incident happens—an authority figure is creepy with a child, a man is aggressive with a younger woman, a white woman touches the hair of a Black woman while giving a "compliment." This incident doesn't rise to the level of assault or rape or any legal definition. But something is most definitely off. The interaction is decidedly non-consensual and contains unwanted sexualization, objectification and/or entitlement.

Like clockwork, when the incident is reported, someone almost always asks a variation on, "Why didn't you say anything?" (Why didn't you tell them off? Why didn't you fight back? *Why didn't you say no?*)

MARCIA

When I hear stories like this, I want to give the long answer: that most of us have had our No undermined in a thousand ways that are almost imperceptible as they are happening. Yet we internalize it, and unless we've had excellent modeling, support and practice, it becomes extremely difficult to say no to things that we don't want happening to our bodies.

Within the realm of consent education, when we talk about "feeling safe to say no," we are talking about so much more than a threat of violence. Threats—explicit, implied, or perceived—are certainly a factor in limiting our ability to say no, but the truth is our issues with saying no start long before then.

In Chapter 5, we talked about the Gatekeeper model of permission, which is what many people's concept of "consent" is based on. Person A wants The Thing (sex, touch, closeness, whatever), and

Person B's job is to just say yes or no. And while getting permission is a far better approach than simply taking action on another's body, the Gatekeeper model has some serious limitations. One of them is that it depends on people's capacity to say no.

This Gatekeeper model is happening inside a larger culture of coercion, which constantly undermines and dismisses people's No, particularly with young people. Authoritarian parents, teachers, and religions teach children that No is an unacceptable response.

This training and socialization, plus power differentials, manipulation, actual and perceived threats of violence, and the body's autonomic freeze response just begin to scratch the surface of the myriad reasons why saying no can be hard for many people. Furthermore, sometimes we appease others because it feels like the only option we have.

It's about more than just *saying* no

This undermining of the No affects more than just your capacity to *say* no. It affects your ability to even *notice* the body's signals that something is not okay with you. When the people around you and your cultural stories consistently model that what you are supposed to do is to bypass any preferences or boundaries, you learn to internalize that those things don't matter. In a culture of coercion, it becomes a survival skill to learn how to tolerate or endure being treated as a means to someone else's ends. Finding your own boundaries, preferences, or pleasure is not even on the table. When *being* a No is not an option, *saying* "no" becomes impossible and the so-called "consent" that is given is empty.

This is why I get so angry when people ask, "Why didn't you say no?"

In Consent Culture, we make room to notice the No, both in ourselves and in others. We learn how to receive a No as information, not rejection. And we proactively create safety and reassurance when someone is a No and says so. These things are absolutely crucial for the development of noticing a No, feeling appropriately entitled to your own No and then saying it.

CULTURAL VALUES MATTER

Many cultures value personal sacrifice for the good of the family or the community over all else. Western culture tends to value individualism. Each of these systems has benefits and shortcomings.

In a culture that values the group over the individual, members may have built-in safety and belonging. Resources are frequently shared freely within the group. People are considered "good" if they are generous, helpful, dependable, and attentive to the needs of others. At the same time, members may lose their sense of self or be railroaded into doing things that make them miserable. Standing out or excelling might be harshly punished.

In a culture where the individual is valued above all else, uniqueness, autonomy and self-sufficiency are praised. At the same time, isolation and alienation are common.

In an ideal world, we would have a perfect balance of belonging and connection with the family and community, while maintaining a robust and engaged sense of self. In reality, what we need as individuals may come into conflict with what the family or group wants. It can be very hard to say no when this happens.

SHOULD THEY BE EVEN ASKING?

We want to be clear that all the exercises and scenarios that we offer in this book are based on the assumption that we are talking about interactions between people who have similar positions of power in the world. Outside a controlled workshop setting, it can get more complicated.

Absolute equality between two individuals is rare, and proximity to power is determined by an intersection of many variables. When there is an inherent power imbalance between two people, it makes it difficult-to-impossible for the person with less power to meaningfully consent to the interaction. Sometimes we have social power that we may not realize we have, so it's imperative that we understand the various ways in which this can manifest.

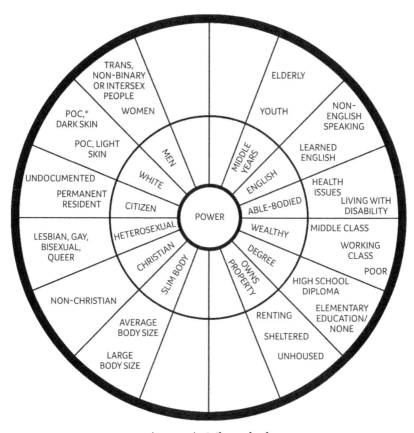

A power/privilege wheel

*POC: People of Color

This is known as a power/privilege wheel. Contrary to what many people think, power and privilege are not things you either have or you don't. Instead, we can have proximity to power in one area of our lives and less access in another area. It's not a competition for who is more powerful or more oppressed, but rather the wheel is a means for understanding the complex intersections of power that affect our interactions.

A power/privilege wheel is a really great tool for self-reflection around all the ways we can be either in proximity to power, or marginalized, or somewhere in between. It's especially helpful for people who are confused about the concept of privilege. At the end of this chapter, we provide some optional questions for participants if you have time for a discussion regarding the power/privilege wheel. We also have a full-page version in Appendix 6, should you want to copy it and hand it out for an exercise.

If one person is in a position to intimidate, reward, or otherwise coerce the other without even trying (such as an employer, teacher, supervisor, or authority figure), then that person should not be requesting touch or even suggesting they would like to be touched by the person with less access to power. Furthermore, they should be mindful of the ways they may feel unconsciously entitled to crowd, talk over, touch or otherwise disregard the bodily autonomy of others. These unconscious expressions of power can make it hard for others to say no.

NOTICING THE FAWN RESPONSE

Throughout this book, we talk about people-pleasing behaviors and how many of us are conditioned to use these as a defense mechanism. Another name for this is a "fawn response."

Unlike "fight, flight or freeze," which we discussed earlier, the fawn response is a *learned* trauma response in which a person reverts to people-pleasing to diffuse conflict and re-establish a sense of safety. The fawn response emerges as a survival skill in response to abandonment, childhood abuse, or domestic violence. It is a mechanism of appeasement to deflect danger, real or perceived.

Many people on the receiving end of a fawn response may misinterpret it as sincere admiration or even as desire, rather than as the trauma response/survival strategy that it is. Others may become uncomfortable or anxious as they are placated. Still others become confused by what is happening in the interaction.

The intense people-pleasing reaction of the fawn response can make it very difficult to both say and hear a No.

HOW CAN WE LEARN TO RECOGNIZE MANIPULATION?

Manipulation is another reason why it can be hard to say no. This is why in the workshop we include a visual demonstration of what consensual interaction does and does not look like. The only learning tool more effective than a visual demonstration is an interactive exercise, but we don't want participants practicing non-consensual exercises, except in the playful and non-threatening way we deal with recognizing our authentic choices in a later chapter. However, some people will need to see things identified as consent violations in order to recognize them in their own lives.

ERICA

Over and over I have young people tell me about an incident or encounter that bothered them, and when I tell them that what happened was actually a consent violation or an attempt at one, they are amazed, because as soon as I say it out loud they recognize it and wonder why they couldn't see it before. The truth is that they didn't see it clearly because manipulation and disrespect of boundaries are so normalized that we are either unable to see it, are numb to it, or even mistake it for romance.

There are two very short demos of what consent does *not* look like, one at this point in the workshop, and one at the very end. We have had some very powerful feedback about how these simple demos can help people prepare for real-life situations. You can change the statements to be true to life for your participants. If you have an assistant you can act out these scenarios with them, or you can just say the statements to an imaginary person.

WORKSHOP EXERCISE

> We've all had the experience of having someone argue with us when we say no. But when it is about your choices around your body and touch, the attempts to argue with you or manipulate you may be quite sneaky. Here are some real-life examples of people NOT honoring or accepting a clear No.

If you have an assistant, act this out with them or talk to the broom or other similar prop. If you are a theatrical person, you can be more entertaining by giving a different character and voice to each of these statements.

> What do you mean, "No"? What, you think you're all that?

> You're so mean! You really hurt my feelings when you said no.

C'mon…just one kiss!

You're no fun! So cold.

Say the next statement with emphasis.

The more that someone argues against or does not accept your No, the more they are sending you red flags that they are not a safe person.

And while we are on the subject, let's dispel the myth that most unsafe people will seem creepy or look threatening. The fact is that most serial predators are charming, charismatic people who are good at manipulating people into doing what they want. Otherwise, they would be a one-time predator, not a serial predator.

Most attempts at manipulation are intended to put you in a position where you feel as if you have to defend your No, your character, or both. When it comes to your personal, physical autonomy, "No" is a complete sentence and you don't need to defend or justify your choice. You are allowed to walk away without saying anything more. You're not a bad person for saying no and disappointing someone. Life is full of disappointments and they will get over it.

Deliver this line for comedic effect.

For example, I'm disappointed right now that [insert celebrity crush here] hasn't realized that we are soulmates, but I've learned to live with it.

So, we're learning why it's important to make others feel comfortable to say no, and now let's look at why we should genuinely appreciate another person saying no to us.

If we are the one asking, it can spare us a lot of confusion and self-doubt when people are clear about their boundaries. No is important information for everyone involved. Please get into your pairs again. A, your job is to ask for a hug, and B, your job is to say no to the hug, but without using the words "no" or "not," or shaking your head.

You may have to go over these instructions a couple of times. People often need to double-check what they're not allowed to say or do.

> Okay great. Let's trade places and do it again please.

It will probably take 30 seconds to a minute for each person to have a chance to play both roles. There is usually laughter.

> Thanks for doing that. How did that feel? When you were asking for the hug, did you wish that the other person could just say no?

Encourage discussion on the take-aways from this exercise as time allows.

For those of you who struggle to say no, remember how good it feels to get a clear answer. Having the ability to give a clear authentic No means that your Yes is more meaningful and heartfelt.

Also, if you have a hard time saying no, remember that every time you say no to one thing you are saying yes to another. No to a party could be Yes to a movie with a good friend. No to spending time with a friend could be Yes to more time learning an instrument. In fact, every No contains an infinity of possible Yes's.

Many cultures value personal sacrifice for the good of the family or the community over all else. Other cultures value individualism. When your family or community wants something from you, it can be hard to say no. Saying no may be harder or easier for you to begin with, but most of us can use more practice.

I'd like everyone to get up and walk around the room please. When you find yourself in front of someone, pair off and take turns asking for a hug and saying no. This time I want you to respond graciously to hearing no and use different wording. You could say things like, "Thank you for being clear," or, "Thanks for knowing your boundaries." Find a way to thank people that feels right for you.

Thanks for doing that. On to the next section!

OPTIONAL DISCUSSION TOPIC

If you have time, have the participants look at the power/privilege wheel provided in Appendix 6. If you copy the wheel and hand it out, you can have the participants draw a line through the different sections of the wheel where they feel they reside in each section. It's important to make this exercise of marking the wheel optional, or tell students that it's okay not to share what they mark on their wheels if they don't want to. We have left some sections blank for participants to come up with their own categories. Some other aspects to consider might be:

- Mental health

- Neurodiversity

- What school you go to

- Employment status.

This wheel was designed to show the dominant culture in the United States. Some categories of the placements would be different in other countries or vary across cultures.

It's less about the students getting their placement on the wheel "right" and more about the experience of looking at some of these things, perhaps for the first time. The process of placing themselves on the wheel should not be graded or judged, but rather used as a jumping off point for discussion.

Some questions you could ask participants about the power/privilege wheel include:

- What is another section that you think could be added to this wheel?

- Did anyone have any "aha!" moments while doing this exercise?

- Can anyone think of some examples of privileges that come with being in close proximity to power in this section of the wheel? (*Point to one section of wheel.*) How about this other section? (*Point to another section.*)

SUMMARY

To recap, we have talked a little more about what consent does *not* look like, and about manipulation and predatory behavior. We have talked about how people who care about us want to have clear information about our Yes's and No's, and we did another exercise to demonstrate a "fuzzy" No. We covered four interpersonal reasons why saying no can be challenging: cultural values, power differentials, the fawn response, and manipulation. We have talked more about why participants' authentic choices are important, how their No is important information to everyone involved, and some of the benefits of being able to clearly communicate a No. We ended with one more exercise to practice saying and honoring no.

Chapter 7

What if I'm a Maybe?

ERICA

Just a few weeks ago I asked my good friend if she wanted to go with me to a show.

"Maybe..." She said uncertainly, "I'm not sure if I can..." Her face was pinched up in a pained and thoughtful expression.

"If you're not sure, just say no," I said. "I have no expectations. Just let me know if you decide you want to go." Her face smoothed out and she broke into a big relieved smile.

I knew exactly what she was feeling. I used to be the kind of person who always said maybe when I really meant no. I had such a hard time saying no that I thought I could forever avoid it by saying maybe when confronted with a request. But all I was really doing was postponing the inevitable. I would live with a cloud of angst and dread hanging over my head, because eventually I would have to either do the thing I didn't want to do, or else finally say the oh-so-difficult No.

The only upside was the extra time it afforded me to come up with a creative and believable excuse. I felt it was best to have an excuse that involved me being previously scheduled to do something extremely unpleasant in the service of someone else. That way, the person I was saying no to couldn't be upset with me, because they would be too busy sympathizing with my unfortunate circumstance.

It certainly never occurred to me that I could just say no and have no explanation for why I was saying it!

I would live with all the mental stress of something hanging over my head until the last possible moment, when I would deliver my sad "I guess no," followed by the elaborate pity-inducing excuse and a quick exit. So painful.

That is why when I learned that one of the rules of Cuddle Party is "When you're a Maybe, say no," It completely rocked my world.

Whaaat?!?! This was the exact opposite of what I usually did! But once I learned the logic and tried it out, I was rocketed to the next level of my boundary evolution. I quickly discovered that saying no instead of maybe, followed with "I'll let you know if I change my mind" freed my mind and spirit. No more dark cloud of anxious anticipation and no more time (and integrity!) wasted formulating excuses.

Saying no was an immense relief. I had new vistas of mental and emotional space. I had time to consider what I really wanted. I could still change my mind to a Yes and it would be a pleasant surprise. Or I could counter offer with a suggestion that was more to my liking. I think my first weeks of practicing this new way of responding made me feel as if the clouds had parted, the sun was peeking out, and little cartoon birds were landing on my shoulders and singing sweetly.

But there was more! I was also learning that saying no is the best course of action when I truly was a Maybe. If I actually didn't know whether I wanted to say yes or no, I could default to a No, and give myself that same mental space. Not only that, but it also gave more freedom to the person making the request. Instead of waiting to find out whether I was a Yes or a No, they could carry on figuring out what to do or who to ask because I was not an option. And if I changed my mind and that was still what they wanted, it would be a nice surprise. Much clearer and kinder than making them continue to ask me after my initial Maybe, and making them wait for an answer.

Defaulting to a No gives me time and space to figure out what I want. There are many ways and techniques to help you figure out what you really want when you're not sure, such as making a list of pros and cons, flipping a coin and seeing if you're happy with the side that lands up, consulting a psychic, or polling your social media followers.

The experience of "being a Maybe" in the face of someone else's request or invitation is multi-faceted. It is often the case that a clear-cut Yes or No is not available to us in a given moment. Here are four of the most common ways Maybe can show up, and some ways to get clarity around each:

- Saying Maybe when you're really a No.

- Not being able to tell what's really true for you.

- The Habitual Yes.

- The fuzziness of "want," "willing" and "enthusiastic."

SAYING MAYBE WHEN YOU'RE REALLY A NO

MARCIA

In 2004, around the time Cuddle Party got started, I was in my mid-twenties and living in New York City. Like a lot of twenty-somethings, I spent a good amount of time in clubs and bars. Unlike most people my age, I started to become a keen observer of my peers' dating and mating habits. It was endlessly fascinating to me: the dressing up, the posturing, the ways people played out gendered expectations. There were so many cultural nuances, from how the Wall Street guys did things, to the bridge-and-tunnel crowd, to the pick-up artists, to the gay bars.

Whether it was a dive bar or an upscale club, one pattern remained the same: A man asks a woman if he can buy her a drink. She looks slightly uncomfortable and says, "Maybe later." After a bit more back and forth, he leaves. A little while later, he comes back. "How about that drink?" She still looks uncomfortable, but she doesn't say no. Sometimes she says okay. Sometimes she repeats her "Maybe later." Sometimes she scans the room nervously for her friend.

Over and over, I would see women not say no to the proffered drink, even when it was obvious (to me) that she wanted to say no.

Now, there are plenty of good reasons for that. Maybe she didn't know if she would be safe saying no. Maybe she didn't have experience in the past of men respecting a No. Maybe (like me) she was raised in the South and was taught it was rude to say no when someone offered her something. Maybe she didn't know how to handle someone expressing attraction to her. Saying no is hard.

But what struck me is how frequently it happened. And how many men did not take the Maybe for a No (especially those Wall Street guys and pick-up artists).

The trouble with saying maybe is that it's a non-answer. It leaves the interaction incomplete and uncertain. Everyone is left unclear about what was meant, what happens next, and whose responsibility it is to take the next step.

"Maybe" might seem like a kindness, but it's really a trap.

NOT BEING ABLE TO TELL WHAT'S TRUE FOR YOU

While saying maybe when you actually mean no is extremely common, it's also quite common to simply not know what you want. This can happen to anyone, depending on the circumstances. It is especially common when children grow up in chaotic, abusive, or authoritarian households, religions, or communities, when they are expected to adhere tightly to specific gender roles, when they are on the receiving end of racialized stereotypes, or when they are parentified in their family dynamics.

These young people grow up to be adults who can't tell what they want, who have a hard time setting boundaries, and who struggle with perfectionism or rebellion against the rigid or chaotic structures they grew up with. They frequently second-guess themselves because they were taught to listen to everything outside themselves and not to their own boundaries, preferences, needs, or wants.

This kind of self-doubt is particularly insidious because predatory people can usually sense it and often exploit it, compounding both trauma and the internal sense of self-doubt.

It's important to realize that this kind of self-doubt doesn't come out of nowhere. Even young people who have relatively stable and supportive home lives are still swimming in the culture of coercion we outlined in Chapter 2 and expanded on in Chapter 6.

A common misconception about self-doubt is that it is a feeling, or a thought. But in our experience, self-doubt can become a *way of being*.

A person who has been repeatedly subjected to abuse, chaotic environments, authoritarianism, sexism, racism, classism, ableism, homophobia, and so on, whether on a personal or systemic level, will internalize some of these messages:

- "You don't know what you're doing and you'll never get it right."

- "Your feelings are dramatic or incorrect."

- "Your existence is inconvenient or inconsistent with how the world *should* be."

- "Other people's wants are more important than your needs."

- "You're not to be trusted if you deviate from what everyone else is doing."

- "You aren't good enough."

- "Your wants don't matter."

- "Your needs don't matter."

- "Who you *are* is broken."

When this happens, it's not a surprise that young people and adults alike don't have the skills to evaluate their boundaries, what they want, how they feel about something or what to do in a situation.

This can show up in a number of ways:

- Perfectionism: "I have to get it right or not do it at all." Not taking healthy risks you want to take for fear of failure.

- Looking outside yourself for the "correct" way to be.

- Overriding your own internal intuition, judgment or integrity.

- Avoiding success or visibility out of fear of being punished or having it taken away.

- Not trusting your experience when something feels bad to you— looking to the law or outsiders to validate that something isn't okay, even when you can tell it feels wrong.

- Not knowing how to discern what you want. Doubting that what you want is the "right" thing, or struggling to make decisions.

For those who have a hard time with this kind of self-doubt, having a non-judgmental space to notice a boundary, preference or need can be a powerful experience. Gentle encouragement to say no (as Erica mentioned in her story above) can be a profound gift.

THE HABITUAL YES

Many people automatically default to saying yes to just about any request. Before there's even a chance to digest what the question was, that Yes is flying out of their mouth. But when No is not an option, a Yes becomes meaningless.

This "Habitual Yes" might happen for many reasons: a desire to please, an inclination to be a workhorse, or from a belief that you're not allowed to take a break or disappoint someone. Frequently, a habit of reflexively saying yes without consideration for yourself is a learned response to relational trauma. But, regardless of its origin, saying yes without considering if that is even true for you has an insidious effect on relationships of all kinds. When it is impossible to say no *within* a relationship, you end up having to say no *to* the relationship.

The Habitual Yes limits our capacity to notice hesitation, uncertainty or Maybes of any kind. It limits our ability to make adjustments to what we agree to do, leading us to take on more than we can handle.

It's worse when it comes to No. For example, most people, if they were told that by attending a party, they would have to say yes to anyone there and were required to do whatever the other party attendees wanted, they would not agree to go to that party! Yet some of us reflexively say yes to whoever needs or wants something anywhere near us. When you repeatedly and unconsciously say yes across your life, despite some part of you screaming no inside, it can lead to distress, frustration, burnout or even a nervous breakdown.

Many of the exercises in this book allow participants to practice saying no, and help them to feel what it's like to get away from the Habitual Yes, even if it's uncomfortable at first.

THE FUZZINESS OF "WANT," "WILLING" AND "ENTHUSIASTIC"

Earlier we talked about Yes and No. But in human interactions, there is a wide-open field where things aren't so clear-cut as just a straight up Yes or No.

Many people are very confused about what an "enthusiastic" Yes means or why feeling an actual Maybe can be so challenging.

Marcia believes this stems from deep confusion of what we mean by "wanting" something. A common refrain from participants in her sexual communication workshops is "But I only want it if the other person wants it too." While this is a lovely sentiment, it can lead to an undesirable pressure to "want" the same things, rather than being able to negotiate honestly based on where we actually are at. Furthermore, it's not actually true. Each of us wants things, often without awareness of what other people want or what they think of our desires. Then, when we become aware of other people's boundaries, judgments, or simple differences in desires, we walk back our wants. This is often accompanied by a sense of shame. It's as if we don't feel that we are allowed to want something that is different from what other people want. (Usually because at some point, it *wasn't* safe to want something different.)

And it gets even more complicated than that.

Many people believe that if the other person doesn't "want" a thing, then they are actually doing something they "don't want to do," and therefore they are being pressured into doing it. It's as if activities in the world are broken up into only two categories: "Wanted" (and therefore good and valid) and "Unwanted" (and therefore bad and invalid).

While there may be some linguistic truth to this, it doesn't capture an essential aspect of human relating: *a gift*.

A gift is something that you give for no other reason than you want the other person to be happy. A true gift comes with no strings attached, may be big or small, and is motivated by care and generosity.

A good gift is given without negative consequences for the giver. It comes from a place of abundance and spaciousness. Our colleague Betty Martin calls this "wholehearted willingness." In other words, the giver is respectful of and responsible for their limits and boundaries and gives freely within them.

It's the difference between wanting, being willing, and tolerating.

Table 7.1: Comparing wanting/being willing/tolerating

Wanting	Being wholeheartedly willing	Tolerating/Enduring
It's my desire. This is something I like and want, and I am hoping you either want it too, or are wholeheartedly willing to join me.	It's your desire, but I feel good about participating. I'm pretty confident I won't feel resentful about joining you. I'm happy to do something that you want and I'll pay attention to my limits and stop before it feels bad to me.	It's not something I want, and I'm just going along with it. I may not feel that I have a choice.
This is what it might sound like out loud or in your head...		
"OMG I want to go see that movie too!"	"Going to the movies sounds good. I hadn't thought about that one, but sure!"	"I don't really want to watch a movie. I'd rather be outside, but I don't want to upset them, so I guess I'll say yes to the movie."
"Yes! I've been wanting to look for a bathing suit at Target. Let's go!"	"I don't really need anything from Target but spending time with you sounds good. Sure!"	"I'm afraid of what will happen if I say no, so I guess we're going to Target."
"Let's hug it out!"	"You seem sad. Would you like a hug?"	"You want to hug me, so here we are."
"Will you give me a massage?"	"Would you like a massage? How much pressure do you like? How is this feeling to you?"	"Is this supposed to feel good? That's kind of intense, but I'll just ride it out. I don't want them to think they're doing a bad job. It'll be over soon."

Looking at the chart above, you can see that while the second and third columns might both register as a Maybe, they are fundamentally different. In the second column, it might not be your desire to do the activity, but you are *enthusiastically willing* to. You can say yes, knowing that you won't be sad, angry, or resentful about it. You can give a wholehearted response of yes, without stress or strain, even if it's not *your* desire.

This middle space is characterized by enthusiasm, spaciousness, and finding some kind of common ground of desire, even if they aren't exactly the same. It is not stretching, reaching, or trying to convince yourself to want something you don't want. It is positively motivated, that is, motivated by a desire *for* something.

Whereas the third column is the kind of Yes borne out of fear, coercion or a lack of belief in one's own autonomy. It's a Yes that is tolerating, enduring and going along with things. It's the kind of Yes that comes from feeling as if there are no good options and it will garner sadness, resentment, or anger down the road. It is negatively motivated, that is, motivated by a desire to avoid a bad outcome, rather than a desire towards or for something in and of itself. This kind of Yes is what's known as "empty consent."

CHECKING-IN EXERCISES

In this section of the workshop, we begin with telling the participants about the beauty of defaulting to a No when they are a Maybe.

Then we share a couple of tools of mindful body scanning in order to determine whether we are a Yes or a No when we're really not sure. Don't forget to personalize it to be authentic to you.

WORKSHOP EXERCISE

I used to be the kind of person who always said maybe instead of no, just to avoid the discomfort of saying no to someone. Then I would go home and stress out about still having to either say no or do the thing that I didn't want to do. I would live under a cloud of anticipation until finally resolving the situation at the last minute.

Now if I'm not sure whether I'm a Yes or No, I default to No and give myself the space and time to figure out what I really want. If I go home and decide I was actually a Yes, I can always change my mind. It's easier to change a No to a Yes than to change a Yes to a No, although either is fine. Being free to change your mind as your situation changes means you're listening to your inner wisdom.

If you're a
Maybe,
say No.

But what if you've thought about it and you still really can't tell if you are a Yes or a No? And sometimes you need to know right away. There might be a couple of reasons for this.

One reason is that there are at least three different kinds of enthusiastic Yes's:

— The first is that you really want something.
— The second is that you aren't sure if you want it, but you are excited to try it and find out if you like it.
— The third is that someone else wants it and you are wholeheartedly willing to give it to them. Like a gift.

This last type of Yes is different from tolerating, enduring, or going along with something. If it feels that you are tolerating something happening to you, that's a No.

The second reason you might not know if you are a Yes or a No is something I call the Habitual Yes. That's when we find ourselves saying yes before we've even had a chance to think about the question, as if it were unthinkable that we might say anything else. When saying yes has become a habit, it takes practice to change, just like breaking any bad habit.

Being aware of why you're saying yes will help you to have clearer boundaries.

Next are two different exercises to help the participants to feel into their bodies, their Yes and their No. You can choose one, or do both. The first one involves the participants getting up and moving around the room, while the second has them sitting still.

Option 1: Active

We're going to try a quick exercise in feeling into your body when you're feeling Yes and when you're feeling No. I'd like everyone to get up and walk around the room looking for objects that make you feel like saying Yes. Objects only, and not other people or anything that they're wearing or carrying. When you find one, look at that object and notice how you feel in your body. Say Yes to the object.

After a couple of minutes, have them do the same thing with an object that is a No for them.

Now please walk around until you find an object that makes you feel No. Say No to the object. Look at it for a bit and notice how your body feels.

Option 2: Seated

I'm going to take you on a little guided meditation now. Please sit up straight, and if it helps you to visualize, close your eyes. Take a deep breath into your belly. Breathe in through your nose and breathe out through your mouth. With your next deep breath, feel your face and neck relax [long pause]. As you breathe deeply feel your shoulders and back relax [long pause]. Feel your breath going down into your belly as your arms and hands loosen [long pause]. As you take another deep breath, feel your legs relax and your feet sink into the floor [long pause]. As you sit comfortably with your muscles in a relaxed position, notice how your body feels. As I guide you to explore different feelings, keep noticing your body. Do your shoulders hunch up? Does your belly tighten? Does it become harder to breathe? Easier?

Continue to breathe deeply and think about something that makes you angry or upset.

[Pause] How does your body feel now?

[Pause] Now think about something that makes you happy or excited.

[Pause] How does your body feel now?

Open your eyes now. Could you feel the difference in your body between the positive and the negative statements? If so, what did it feel like?

Other possible questions are:

> - "What do you think about saying no when you're not sure about something?"
> - "Did you feel Yes and No in different parts of your body?"
> - "How do you feel when you ask someone to do something, and they say maybe?"
> - "Any other 'aha!' moments to share?"
> - "Did anyone fall asleep?"

OPTIONAL DISCUSSION TOPIC

If you have extra time, and it's appropriate for your group, help your participants to make their own table of situations in which the person saying yes is saying it because they are wanting it, willing to do it, or tolerating it. You can use examples from the table above to prompt them.

Here are some questions you could ask participants to explore this chapter's themes further:

- What are some clues that someone might be saying maybe when they are a No?

- What are some clues that someone might be habitually saying yes, rather than considering their actual preferences?

- What are some ways you can support your friends or classmates to say no when it seems as if they might need help with it?

- How can you tell the difference in yourself between being whole-heartedly (or enthusiastically) willing to do something versus kind of going along with it and tolerating it? How do these feel different to you?

SUMMARY

To recap, we've talked about why we sometimes say maybe when we mean no, and how that can cause problems for everyone. We also went over the situation of not being able to tell what is true for us, and why many of us find ourselves in that situation quite often. We looked at defaulting to Yes when we are really a Maybe, or even a No, and how for many of us automatically saying yes has become a bad habit. We also went over the grey area of being enthusiastically willing, even if the thing we're saying yes to is not our own desire.

Chapter 8

Changing Your Mind

In Consent Culture, you are allowed to change your mind about any kind of interaction that involves your bodily autonomy.

In our current reality, this aspect of bodily autonomy is not always respected. A culture of coercion would like you to believe that you cannot change your mind, even about your own body. But that's not true.

OUTDATED IDEAS

When we were teenagers (Erica in Canada in the 1980s and Marcia in Georgia in the 1990s), there was a prevailing societal message that a girl should not make out with a boy unless she was prepared to "go all the way," because boys and men have needs that must be met. (The subtext was that it was a woman's and girl's job to meet those needs, with no thought to *their* needs.) We picked up the message that men could be physically damaged by becoming excited and then having to stop.

We don't remember any positive messaging about female pleasure or about women having sexual desires or needs. Women who liked sex were "nymphos" or "sluts." There was also near-total silence in the mainstream media about same-sex relationships until the early 1990s. Mainstream society was so ignorant of queer culture that an entire generation of straight men proudly wore Queen t-shirts, oblivious to the meaning of the word.

Ancient history. A lot has changed in the past 40 years. Now the conversation includes a spectrum of genders, orientations, and relationship styles. There is more and more discussion about the importance of female sexual pleasure. The messaging is beginning to be more diverse and equitable.

And unfortunately, some damaging beliefs still persist. Shockingly, as recently as 2019 there was a North Carolina law rooted in these beliefs that stated that no rape was committed if a person initially agreed to sex.[31] What that law was doing was not recognizing a person's right to change their mind. Many recent discussions with young people, and older people alike, have convinced us that this toxic belief persists in many forms.

Younger women have told us that they still have feelings of obligation to meet their partners' sexual desires regardless of whether or not they want to. This happens in both dating and relationship situations. If they refuse to meet the entitled expectations of their partners, they report facing a backlash of shaming and retaliation.

More disturbingly, younger women have described to us brutal instances of rape, and then said that they didn't believe that it was rape, because they had initially agreed to have sex. Or because they went to his house. Or because he was their boyfriend at the time. They themselves don't believe that they have the right to change their minds. They believe that certain situations obligate them to perform sexual acts, regardless of their own feelings and desires.

And it's not just women who feel obligated. Many boys and men have described to us that they feel pressured to want sex all the time, regardless of their actual desires. And girls and women often enforce brutal gender norms around men's sexuality, both in their roles as mothers and in their roles as sexual partners.[32]

At least one in six men have reported being sexually assaulted during their lives, most often by other men.[33] But it is also frequently the case that men are pressured, coerced, and assaulted by women and then are afraid to talk about it even with their closest friends. They fear that they will be mocked, as has happened in the past.[34] Many people believe that men cannot be sexually assaulted by women, but this is patently false.[35]

In a culture of coercion, a sense of entitlement is one part of the equation. Another part of the equation is a corresponding sense of disempowerment and lack of entitlement to one's own bodily autonomy or personal space.

The belief that we cannot change our minds once something physical has started leads to many experiences that may not be assault or even harassment, but still cause harm.

Early on in Cuddle Party, Marcia realized that she had to make this principle explicitly a rule: "You are allowed to change your mind." Otherwise people would end up staying awkwardly in a cuddle position, even as their arm fell asleep or they wanted to go to the bathroom, waiting for that mythical moment when the other person was "done." It was especially awkward when two people both waited for the other, when in reality each of them would have changed positions or done something different far sooner if they just felt that they were allowed to.

Many of us got into trouble as young people for changing our minds, whether it was from our parents about not wanting to hug a relative that we used to hug, or from an early partner who pressured us into "following through" on a sexual encounter. Undoing this early conditioning is an important part of building Consent Culture.

Even in long-term, loving relationships, problems arise around changing boundaries. For example, a bad week at work can lead to a significant change in interests and boundaries even for a much-anticipated romantic weekend away. Or, as our bodies and emotions change through life, we may want more affection from our loved ones—or no contact at all. Some women may have completely different boundaries around their bodies being touched when they are pregnant or when they are breastfeeding, which may be hard for their partners to understand. When people doubt their own right to shift their boundaries, it can lead to communication breakdowns within their relationships. When you feel as if you can't change your mind about what happens with your body, it can lead to resentment, frustration, and anger.

Sometimes people have a hard time understanding and expressing their own changing boundaries. They may have feelings of discomfort or resentment and not even be aware of what is causing them. We all need to practice the skill of examining our feelings and discovering their origins. Sometimes the discomfort or resentment is a clue that our boundaries have changed but we haven't communicated it. We all need to practice knowing and communicating our boundaries, as they shift. And, we need to normalize the idea that our boundaries and desires will change, sometimes quickly.

In Consent Culture, once we do figure out and express that our boundaries have changed, our partners will hear and honor us. It doesn't necessarily mean they like it, but they respect that you have the right to change your mind. Presently, many people feel entitled to shame and denigrate those who change their minds, or do not meet entitled expectations.

Learning to gracefully handle not getting what you want is part of building Consent Culture too.

NO MATTER WHEN, NO MATTER WHERE, NO MATTER WHY

In Consent Culture, you can always change your mind and it's normal to do so. Consent is given moment to moment according to changing circumstances, feelings, and intentions.

Because for many people, unabashedly changing your mind may feel entirely new, it's important that we emphasize this.

WORKSHOP EXERCISE

I want to stress how important it is to know that you always have the right to change your mind during personal interactions. You are NOT signing a contract when you decide to spend time with someone, kiss them, touch them, or any other activity. Even if you are in a relationship and living with someone, or even married to them, you still have the right to have changing boundaries, from moment to moment. Just because you wanted to do something yesterday, or five minutes or even five seconds ago, does not mean that you should want to do it again right now.

You can always change your mind.

In the next bit, Erica talks about how her personal boundaries have changed with a demonstration that usually helps people visualize their boundaries and how they can change. You will have to find a way to describe this boundary strategy that suits you.

The reality is that we often don't know exactly where a boundary is until right after it is crossed. I used to be the kind of person who trusted people too much, too quickly and I kept my boundaries close like this, so that when they were crossed I would be hurt.

Hold your arms in front of you in a semicircle with your hands close to your chest and then use one hand to show how crossing that line immediately impacts your chest.

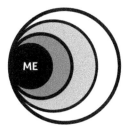

Visual demonstration of boundary zones

Table 8.1: Boundary zones

Dark grey	Light grey	White
• Boundaries too close to limits. • Other people's wants matter more than my needs. • When my boundaries are crossed, I get hurt. • Over-giving.	• Discernment zone. • Listening for how respectful others are of my boundaries. • Adjusting in or out, based on real-time information. • Some people allowed closer, others kept away.	• Boundaries too far out. • Default to mistrust. • Not letting people in at all. • Boundaries so far out that I lose intimacy.

> Over time I have learned to keep my boundaries further out, so that when they are crossed I am still okay.

Move the semicircle further out from your body, so that this time when you use one hand to demonstrate crossing that line it is far enough from your chest that it doesn't make contact.

> Depending on how well I know the person, or how safe I feel, I can move my boundaries further out, or closer in.

Use your semicircle of arms to demonstrate moving a midway boundary closer in, then further out. For a laugh, you can orient yourself towards someone and in a joking way put your arms out as far as possible with an exaggerated look on your face. Only do this if you're confident you can pull it off in a way that's funny and doesn't hurt anyone's feelings.

This business of feeling into your body, and noticing what it feels like to say or do the opposite of what you actually want, takes practice, so we're going to lead on to another exercise that helps participants do that in a fun way. You'll be splitting them into groups of three, but if the numbers are wrong, one or two groups of four will still work. If you do have a group of four, let them know that their individual turns will be a little shorter.

> Okay, we're going to do a fun exercise to practice what we've just learned. For this exercise, we're going to split up into groups of three. Once you're in your group of three, pick someone to be the first No person.

Once everyone is divided up and the No people have been chosen, continue on.

> Okay, No person, your job is to say no to everything. No matter how much you want to say yes, you have to say no. The other two people in the group, your job is to ask the No person things that make it hard to say no to. An example could be, "Can I give you some money?" or, "Would you let me do your chores for you?" Don't ask about anything to do with sex or violence please. If you are the No person, remember to check in with how your body is feeling when you say no to something you would rather say yes to. Okay, you can start now please.

After a minute or so get them to switch to another No person. If you have groups of four, approach that group a little sooner and get them to switch. After another minute or so, repeat the process so that everyone in each group gets a turn as the No person. There is usually a lot of laughter during this exercise.

> Great. Thanks for doing that. We're going to do that again except this time the No person is a Yes person. This time it is your job to say yes to everything. You're not going to DO anything, but you have to say yes. The other two, your job is to ask questions that make it hard for the Yes person to say yes. An example could be, "Will you listen to some poetry I just made up?" or, "Could I have your cell phone please?" Again, no questions about sex or violence. If you are the Yes person, remember to check in with how your body is feeling when you have to say yes to something you would rather say no to.

Once again get them to change Yes people every minute or so, until everyone has had a turn. Encourage a discussion of what they got out of the last exercise. Some possible questions are:

- "How did it feel to say no when you wanted to say yes?"
- "How did it feel to say yes, when you wanted to say no?"
- "Did you notice any sensations in your body?"
- "Any 'aha!' moments to share?"

OPTIONAL DISCUSSION TOPIC

If you have time for extra discussion and it's appropriate for your group, ask your participants what they feel are their obligations and expectations in an intimate interaction. If relevant, use one or both of the examples below.

For younger participants

"I wanted to hug my auntie when she came to visit, but then she hugged me waaay longer than I was comfortable with. I let go, but she didn't. I could hardly breathe, she was squeezing me so hard. I had to just wait until she let me go, because I didn't know what to say or do."

For older participants

"When I was young, I learned what I thought sex should look like, but nothing about how to say no to what I didn't want, or how to ask for what I wanted. I didn't have very good self-esteem and not a whole lot of knowledge either. When I hooked up with people, I didn't know how to do anything but go along with what the other person wanted, or even how to stop when I wanted to. I did a lot of things I didn't want to do, because I thought once things got started, I had to just go through with it."

Questions

- Let's brainstorm some phrases that feel good to say, in order to let others know that you've changed your mind.

- What are some ways you can let your friends or siblings know that it's okay to change their mind with you?

SUMMARY

In this chapter, we have discussed the importance of being able to change your mind at any time, and how beginning to interact with someone is not like signing a contract. Consent is something given from moment to moment. We've talked about boundaries, how they can shift, and different strategies for creating safety for ourselves with our boundaries. We did more exercises to practice feeling the difference between being a Yes and a No and how it feels in our bodies when we don't express this authentically.

Chapter 9

Consent Is Collaboration

If consent is an agreement about how we'll play or share space together that we continue to make as we go, then collaboration is the means by which we get there. Collaboration requires a few things from us—an awareness that other people might operate differently from us, a non-judgmental curiosity about that difference, and a willingness to take the time to bridge our understandings and clarify assumptions.

MARCIA

Once upon a time, I ran a relationship discussion group for people in non-traditional relationships. Every month, participants would gather to talk about whatever our topic was: commitment, hookups, boundaries, love, sex, attachment, fighting well, relating well, meeting family, the holidays...whatever. Over nine years of meetings, no matter what the topic was, it became obvious to me that a major source of relationship upheaval had to do with a difference in what each person *meant* by their words or actions. What was obvious to one person meant something completely different to the other.

Even in loving relationships where people really want the best for one another, misunderstandings blossom and disagreements fly off the rails because even when both people are using the same words, they attach wildly different meanings to them.

That's why one of my favorite questions to bring into a conversation that is starting to feel adversarial rather than collaborative is "Can you say more about what you mean by that?" Pausing to ask for clarification is an effective way to get on the same page with your friend or partner.

Having awareness that other people might make different assumptions and meanings from you is a valuable skill in creating agreements with others. Working together to find out what those assumptions are is at the heart of collaboration.

COLLABORATING TO FIND SHARED MEANING

The word "negotiation" means different things to different people. For some, it's a word that means carefully stepping through challenging terrain, as in "negotiating our way down the hill." For others, it implies power differentials and a win/lose proposition.

We use the word "collaboration" when referring to creating agreements, instead of "negotiation" to reinforce the idea that we are working together as equals and that this isn't a forced transaction or interaction. Finding the right words to unlock a new paradigm is an important part of creating a new culture. We are digging deep in the unconscious, finding the points where damaging socialization can be unlearned. We can build a worldview based on equality and mutual respect with words that contain those principles.

You'll find this to be true of many words we use in this book and workshop: consent, power, privilege, agreements, bodily autonomy, boundary, limit, and so on. Different words bring up different associations.

As a facilitator, your job is not to force definitions on participants or to require them to agree. You can model collaboration and curiosity by starting a conversation about how different words and actions can have different meanings to different people. Then, you can define words as "how we will use this in this workshop" and leave it optional for how participants might want to use them afterwards.

CURIOSITY IS KEY

Collaboration requires us to check our underlying assumptions and bring curiosity to the table. What is nice about being curious about another person's experience is that you don't have to play guessing games and you don't have to know everything. You can just ask questions.

Checking in: "Hey, it seems as if you might not be good with this. Do you want to stop?"

Meaning: "You said this thing earlier, and as I thought about it, I realized I wasn't sure if we meant the same thing by it. Can you say more about it?"

Input: "What would make this even better for you?"

Assessment: "How are you feeling right now?"

Feedback: "What do you want more of/less of/to be different?"

Support: "What would feel helpful to you right now, if you know?"

Open-ended questions are ideal, but anything you find yourself wondering about, you can ask about, instead of getting caught up in an anxiety loop in your head.

Not everyone means the same thing when they use the same words. Not everyone's nervous system is wired the same way. Not everyone makes the same cultural assumptions. Not everyone has the same trauma history or lack thereof. Not everyone has the same experience of being centered or being othered. People differ in how much closeness they want, how much physical contact they want, and where they perceive themselves to be relative to other people. Curiosity provides a path through friction and disagreement. But it also creates new opportunities for connection that may not have been visible before.

WORKSHOP EXERCISE

In this part of the workshop, you'll begin by reminding participants of what they've learned and practiced already, and then introduce them to the next set of exercises. It looks something like this:

> Alright, so we've practiced saying no and yes and knowing which one we are. We've practiced hearing no and appreciating clarity, and learned about how it's okay to change your mind. Now let's talk about collaboration.
>
> But first, I'm going to ask you all to think of a tree. If you like, you can close your eyes and try to really see it.

Give them a moment to do this.

> Can anybody tell me what kind of tree they thought of? What did you imagine when you thought of a tree? How about you?

Get a sampling of tree visions from the group.

> Before we can collaborate, we have to be able to understand what other people mean when they're talking to us. For instance, the same words can mean different things to different people.
>
> Now, if we are all thinking of such different things when we hear the word "tree," how much more complicated would the differences be if we were talking about words like "love" or "relationship" or "society," or almost any word at all? I'd like you to keep that in mind as we do the next exercise.
>
> We're going to get up and move around and do some greeting exercises now. This can look like shaking hands, fist bumping, hugging, bowing, or waving. Or another kind of greeting of your own creation. If you are too uncomfortable with an exercise or any part of it, just sit it out.
>
> Please get up and walk around the room. Look at the other people walking around the room.

Let them walk around for a minute.

> Now let's all end up standing in front of someone.

Pause until everyone has a partner. If it's an odd number either you or your assistant can be a partner while you are leading, or ask three people to be a group.

> Without saying any words, use your facial expressions and body language to collaborate with your partner to have the most mutually agreeable greeting.

Give them a minute or so until everyone has had a chance to figure out how they will greet each other. There will probably be some laughter but if you hear people talking remind them that you've asked them to do this without speaking.

> Thank you. Now, silently to yourselves, think about what you liked, and what you didn't like about that style of greeting.
>
> Great. Let's walk around the room and look down at other people's feet.

Give them a minute or so to walk around.

> Stop when you find yourself in front of a friendly pair of feet. We're going to greet each other again, except that this time we won't make eye contact or look for body language. We'll keep looking at our feet, and rely entirely on our verbal communication to collaborate to have the most mutually agreeable greeting possible.

Give them a couple of minutes for their greetings. People will be relieved to be able to speak again, but also many will be feeling uncomfortable about not making eye contact, so there will likely be some awkward laughing and a fair bit of talking.

> Great, thank you. Now think about what you liked, and didn't like, about that style of greeting.
>
> All right, let's walk around the room some more and this time you can look at people's faces again.

Give them a minute to walk around looking at each other again.

> Stop when you find yourself in front of someone that you haven't greeted yet. This time we will use all of the skills from the first and second greetings. So, facial expressions, body language, and verbal communication are all used to collaborate on the most mutually agreeable greeting possible.

Give them a couple of minutes to make sure that everyone has a chance to figure out their greeting.

> And now think about what you liked and didn't like about that style of greeting.

At this point you can let everyone sit down again.

> Which kind of greeting was your favorite?

Give a minute for responses. Participants may be trying to argue why one of the greeting exercises was better than the others.

> There is no right or wrong answer to this. Some people even prefer the one where we stare at our feet. Everyone has different communication styles and it's good to know which ones you prefer to use when you're trying to collaborate with someone for a positive interaction. The way others communicate may not be the same way you do, and this can lead to misunderstandings.
>
> Another question: When you were checking in with your greeting partner, how many of you asked the question "Is this okay?"? We want to reach for a higher standard than "okay". If your partner is saying, "Okay" or, "I don't mind" or "I guess" or, "Sure," that's not enthusiastic consent. A good way to avoid miscommunication is to seek enthusiastic consent, and ask questions that have to be answered with full sentences, such as, "What would you like to do?" or, "Tell me what would make you happy."

Encourage discussion on this topic of how miscommunication can happen or has happened to people. Some questions that could be helpful for this include:

> — "What did you notice about yourself during these greeting exercises?"
> — "Which was your favorite style of greeting and why?"(Participants are often amazed to learn that not everyone has chosen the same favorite greeting exercise.)
> — "What else besides different communication styles can cause misunderstandings?"
> — "What are some things we can do to avoid miscommunication?"

OPTIONAL EXERCISE (ALL AGE GROUPS)

If time allows you could go over the basic communication skill of repeating back what you heard and getting confirmation before responding to your partner. You could get them to practice. It looks like this: Partner A: "I like your shirt" (this can be any statement). Partner B: "What I hear you saying is that you like my shirt. Is that right?" Partner A: "Yes, that's what I meant." Partner B: "Cool, thanks!"

Try getting them to gradually move to more complex statements, like, "I'm not sure how I feel right now" so that there is more of a challenge for Partner B in confirming what Partner A is meaning to say.

Practice this kind of listening and confirmation of what is being said for a few minutes. Depending on the time available you can ask more questions about what the participants experienced doing this exercise.

These exercises are all about practicing clear communication in different ways, and experiencing obstacles to communication. Participants realize that communicating isn't always so straightforward and are reminded of the importance of being clear and looking out for miscommunication pitfalls.

SUMMARY

To recap, in this section we have examined the concept of collaborating for consent. We've talked a bit about how different cultures and individuals communicate differently and make meaning differently. We have also explored how curiosity can help us bridge these gaps. We did a series of exercises in order to explore different communication styles and to help participants become more familiar with their own comfort levels around different ways to communicate. We then ended with a tip on how to have more clear communication and get better information from a partner.

Chapter 10

Asking for What You Want Is Hard

ERICA

But what *do* I want?

I remember the first morning as a single mom that I was able to wake up and say to myself, "What do *I* want to do today?" I believe this was several years into my parenting adventures. It certainly wasn't the first morning of my life that I thought that thought, but I'll never forget it, because it was the first time I was conscious of thinking it, and conscious of what a precious gift it was just to be able to ask that question.

I have no doubt that there are many people in the world who have never had one morning in which they could think that thought. Right off the bat, thinking about asking for what you want brings up many questions of power differentials and dynamics. For example, who gets to ask for what they want? And when they do ask, who listens?

Marcia's work on asking for what you want opened up new vistas for me. It has helped me to consider some of the concepts involved in asking for what I want, and all the things that stop me from doing that. Looking back now, I realize that I grew up with very mixed messages about asking for, and getting, what I want.

As a child, I was told by some adults that I could do or have anything, but all around me were women modeling self-sacrifice and self-effacement. Movies and TV portrayed women as objects and accessories, never the hero of the story. I already knew at a young age that when I did ask for something I wanted, I would need to have a justification ready, and be prepared to be disappointed.

Before the age of five, I was somehow effectively and silently taught that my desires were not as important as, for instance, my oldest brother's desires. Actually, I was made to understand that my *needs* were not as important as my brother's, or really any man's, desires. At the same time, I was learning, in the same non-verbal and indirect way and without being conscious of it, that there was a hierarchy in which my desires and needs as a white person were more important than those of people of color.

Knowing what I want, let alone asking for it, has been a struggle throughout my life. It still is, but now I have techniques and practices to help me lean into myself and look more closely. As with much of my personal growth, it comes down to examining biases, both internal and external, and then practicing doing uncomfortable things!

I love Marcia's teachings on desire smuggling. I have probably spent most of my life desire smuggling, because who just asks for what they want?! How many times have I offered a massage because I really wanted to receive one? And then been disappointed because it was not reciprocated. Changing these habits is revolutionary!

Sometimes I'm afraid to ask for what I want, because I fear that others will have a hard time saying no, as I have for most of my life. I worry that they will give me what Marcia calls a "Habitual Yes." I don't want to put others in that same painful position that I have struggled to escape from. That has led me to do a fair bit of double-checking and investigating people's Yes's. Some have found that annoying, but others have found it a relief.

At first, I didn't understand how learning to ask for what you want is really part of Consent Culture, until I started looking at consent as a collaboration. And how can people truly collaborate if the question before them is unclear? It can be unclear whether there is an ask or an offer. It can be unclear who the request is for. It can be unclear what the request even is! And it is certainly very unclear if we don't ask at all, and hope that others will just figure it out.

A mutually beneficial collaboration can only happen when all parties involved are made fully aware of who is asking for what, who wants what, and who is willing and/or enthusiastic. That process *starts* with figuring out what you want. Then comes asking. The next step is knowing what you are enthusiastic about, or willing to try, and giving yourself the time to figure that out.

TOO MUCH, AND NOT GOOD ENOUGH

The world is not friendly to our desires. Putting words to your longings, your fantasies, your crushes, and your curiosities is challenging for most people. There are lots of reasons we don't ask for what we want, including not knowing what we want, not having the language to ask, and not wanting to rock the boat when things are "good enough."

But by and large, the main reason we don't ask for what we want is fear. The fears might be about losing attachment: rejection, humiliation, and judgment. Or they might be fears about not being good enough: disappointment, shame, loss, and guilt. Sometimes the fears are about being too vulnerable: not getting it, or putting too much at stake. Or the fears might be about hurting the other person: they might think *they* aren't good enough and withdraw.

We might fear being seen as asking for too much, or being demanding or "high maintenance." We may be told that we should expect less. Men and boys who are attuned to the harassment many women experience may fear coming across as "one of those men," or as being pushy.

Maybe we've asked for what we want before only to discover that it wasn't what we wanted at all. Maybe it didn't go well for other reasons, and now we worry about that happening again.

Fear rules our desires. Fear can make it impossible to know what we want, or to ask for it. These fears didn't come out of nowhere, either. You know to be afraid of these things because you've experienced them.

Sometimes it's indirect:

- Watching helplessly as a friend gets judged for wanting something that seems just a little "outside the box."

- The look of disdain on an adult's face when someone else expresses interest in something that you also want.

- Seeing people's hearts be torn apart on reality TV.

- Watching others' imperfections be shredded to bits on the internet.

- Seeing others being met with anger or judgment when they dare to ask for something.

Often it's also direct:

- Hearing someone say "Ewww" after you share a vulnerable truth.

- Being laughed at for your youthful eagerness and enthusiasm.

- Being judged harshly for even asking.

- Getting a No that is laden with judgment for you even asking.

- Being told that having that need or want is wrong, silly, or selfish.

- Having someone pull away from you after you go out on a limb to ask for something.

- Being on the receiving end of racist or sexist messaging that you are arrogant or "ungrateful" for asking for what you need or want.

- Being loved conditionally—only if you're smart enough, pretty enough, strong enough or conform enough (especially when "enough" seems to be a moving target).

The world is hostile to the sweet, fumbling, imperfect nature of desire. Sometimes, it's even hostile to *us*. People are judgmental. Some people are celebrated for wanting out loud, while others are punished for it.

And so, to cope, we hide our desires from ourselves and from the people we love. And in the process, we start doing something Marcia calls "desire smuggling."

MARCIA

As I was working with my clients and students around issues of needs, desire, longing, and shame, I found I needed a way to talk about the enormous range of things that people do as a way to avoid the vulnerability of talking about what they want directly. In 2014, I coined the term "desire smuggling" for a workshop I was leading on bedroom communication.

I defined it as "hiding what you really want from yourself and/ or a loved one, while finding covert strategies to get (at least pieces of) what you want."

It resonated immediately with my students. They could see themselves in the ineffective, floundering, sometimes funny ways other students described trying to get what they wanted in relationships. It provided an access point to compassion when they caught themselves undermining their relationships or self-sabotaging. It gave them a way to talk with their loved ones about what was underneath "bad behavior." I always made it clear that it is perfectly acceptable to set boundaries around toxic expressions of desire smuggling. Seeing that we all sometimes make odd or unsavory choices helped to take the edge off their own fears.

WHAT DOES DESIRE SMUGGLING LOOK LIKE?

Desire smuggling is something we all do to avoid vulnerability, even as we still need what we need and want what we want. It's a reasonable response to the noxious pond of shame and judgment we're swimming in.

Desire is powerful. Even in the face of fear, rejection, guilt, and loss, we yearn for things. And consciously or unconsciously, we *will* try to get them. The stakes are often high around what we truly want, and being direct can often seem daunting, or even outright terrifying.

It may feel unsafe to need and want things, but most of us will still try anyway. This isn't necessarily bad, but without understanding that this is how desire and shame work, we can go down some dark paths.

When Marcia teaches about smuggling desire, a class of 20 people can easily come up with 50–80 examples of ways we try to get what we want when we think it's not available. We are endlessly creative in coming up with techniques for smuggling desire.

Table 10.1 shows some of the things you might do.

Table 10.1: Desire smuggling tactics

Mostly harmless, but not necessarily effective	May cause problems in a relationship and/or to self	Toxic and/or antisocial
• Hint about what you want • Find out if the other person wants the thing you want first • Talk about how "a lot of people do it" (instead of saying you want to do it) • Minimize it by saying "just" or "only" • Be loud and bombastic to distract from it • Want the other person to guess • Wait for the right time • Wait for a sign • Obsess about pros/cons • Overthink it • Send videos/links about the thing you want • Talk about it to everyone but the person/people who can give it to you • Tell a story/make art about the thing you desire • Post about it online • Play "options roulette" (where one option you give is the one you secretly want) • Offer to give the thing you want • Substitute something else • Avoid it altogether	• Expect the other person to read your mind • Get drunk/high to remove inhibitions • Emotionally withdraw • Pester the other person to want it • Complain that you don't get it • Be "nice" and hope to be rewarded • Make unspoken deals • Give ultimatums • Tack on obligation to a "gift" • Guilt-trip • Be passive-aggressive • Blame them for not giving it to you • Hope and hope and hope • Settle for not getting it ever • Shame yourself for having that desire • Shame others with the same desire • Spiritually bypass ("It's not good or holy to want that") • Buy into a romance myth ("If you really loved me, you would do X") • Assume they should just *know* • Punish your partner for not giving it to you • Punish yourself/self-harm for wanting it • Make sugar-coated demands • Judge someone asking for what you want • Judge someone for getting what you want	• Bully • Belittle • Show contempt • Maliciously trick or deceive the other person • Use emotional blackmail • Use actual blackmail • Threaten violence • Threaten suicide • Use force • Use violence • Steal • Assault

DESIRE SMUGGLING IS A CLUE

Looking at this list, it's easy to criticize, blame, or shame yourself (or other people) for doing these things. After all, some of these behaviors are extremely antisocial and vile. Some are damaging to relationships. Others are less toxic to other people, but damaging to you. Some are just not terribly effective for getting what you want.

When you catch yourself, or someone you love, smuggling desire, it's an opportunity to bring your curiosity in and notice that that is a *clue* to a desire.

When you catch this clue, you have an opportunity to either be more direct yourself, or help your friend to be more direct with you. By offering a warm and safe haven for them to talk about what is going on for them, you can provide emotional fortification for them to want things that may have seemed taboo before.

When it's safe to have desire, you no longer have to smuggle it.

SOME THINGS TO KEEP IN MIND
You still get to have boundaries

Hearing about someone's desires doesn't obligate you to do anything with that information. Telling someone about what you want doesn't mean they have to fulfill it. It can be enough to just be heard without judgment.

Boundaries generate safety and clear understandings both for ourselves and others. It's much easier to appreciate others sharing what they want when you are confident that you aren't mandated to do those things. And you can be confident that you aren't overstepping when you know the other person has the ability to maintain their own boundaries.

You don't want to pester

Although we always want to honor the No of others, not every No means "No forever and never ask me again." Some Nos are time or situation dependent. It would be a hard, cold world if hearing no meant we could never ask that question of that person ever again. Give some time between asks. A good rule of thumb is to ask no more than twice, then let it go.

A warm and safe haven

You can help others feel more comfortable speaking up by encouraging them to think about what they want, and letting them know that you genuinely want to know about their desires. You can also give them space to talk it through until a desire becomes clearer for them.

It's expected that people will want different things. Even if something isn't your cup of tea, you can still be open-hearted, kind, and respectful when they share with you.

WORKSHOP EXERCISE

So how do we communicate all this to the participants? We offer an exercise to practice encouraging each other to ask for what we want, and we follow it with a preamble like this:

> We've gone over how most people have a hard time saying no, and now we're going to talk about the asking. The truth is, most people also have a hard time asking for what they want.
>
> We have a lot of different reasons for not asking for what we want. Maybe we are scared of feeling vulnerable, or fear being rejected. Maybe we don't want to make others feel pressured. Maybe we are so sure that we can't receive what we want, that we see no point in asking. Maybe we don't spend much time thinking about what we truly want.
>
> But if consent is collaboration, and only one person is asking for what they want, then that is a very limited collaboration. If neither of them is asking for what they want, it's a guessing game! To have an effective collaboration we each need to be comfortable asking for what we want, as well as being comfortable to say no or yes.
>
> Often when we feel uncomfortable to ask for what we want, we do something called "desire smuggling," where we try to get what we want without having to ask. This can range from dropping hints to complex manipulative maneuvers all the way to extremely violent and antisocial behavior. Desire smuggling is natural and common, but it becomes toxic when we're not prepared to honor another person's No.
>
> But a lot of us don't allow ourselves to even think about what we really want. Discovering what we want and learning how to ask for it takes practice.
>
> I'm going to ask you to get into your pairs again, and remember who is A and B, and face each other. A, your job is to ask B, "What do you want?" B, you're going to come up with something you want. It can be ridiculous or totally unrealistic, but it cannot involve sex or violence. Once B says the thing they want, A responds with, "Thanks for letting me know."

Ask for as many things as you can think of for 30 seconds, and I'll tell you when to stop. Go!

Great. Now A and B trade places, so that B is asking, and do that again. Ask for as many things as you can for the next 30 seconds, and Go!

Even if you are already good at asking for what you want, you can play this game with friends to help them get more comfortable with it as well. If you struggle with asking for what you want, you can practice with a friend, until it comes more easily.

Sometimes we ask for something we think we want, and then once we get it we realize we don't really want it. Even if you were the one to ask, you are still allowed to change your mind. And just because you can't figure out exactly what you want at first, it's okay to keep asking until you figure it out.

Here are some possible questions for unpacking the exercise:

— "How did it feel to be asked about what you want?"
— "How did it feel to be thanked for sharing it?"
— "How did it feel to thank someone else for sharing what they want?"
— "Any 'aha!' moments that anyone would like to share?"

OPTIONAL DISCUSSION TOPIC

Have the group brainstorm a list of reasons why people don't ask for what they want.

Then show them Table 10.1 from this chapter that lists the different kinds of "desire smuggling." (You can find a full page printable version of this chart online at creatingconsentculture.com/book-resources using the password "book"; there is also a copy in Appendix 7.)

Now get them to look at the list that they brainstormed side-by-side with the table and have a short discussion about how desire smuggling is a natural reaction to the fears of asking. Talk about how it's normal and common to do desire smuggling, and how these behaviors can be seen as a clue that there is something they are struggling with. Here are some questions you could ask to facilitate a discussion about this:

- Did making these lists give you any "aha!" moments you'd like to share?

- What is one step we could take to get better at asking for what we want?

- What is one step we could take to make it easier for people in our lives to ask for what they want?

SUMMARY

To recap, we have talked about how and why it is hard to ask for what we want, and how this impacts on collaborating for consent. We have discussed desire smuggling, and covered how to create safety for asking in yourself and others. We have done an exercise to practice asking, and encouraging others to ask for what they want. Onwards!

Chapter 11

Like a Deer in the Headlights

ERICA

Over the past few years I have occasionally supplemented my income by driving for rideshare companies. A few years ago, on a sunny Friday morning, I picked up a young man who was dressed for work and seemed quite polite. He sat in the front and we started to make small talk as we headed towards his workplace. We were nearing the destination when I saw something out of the corner of my eye. I looked over and was stunned to see that his penis was out. He wasn't touching himself. It was just out.

For *years*, I had promised myself that the next time a guy tried *anything* like this I would yell and fight and do something about it. But that's not what happened.

I froze. I drove in complete silence. It felt like my conscious self had left the car and I was suddenly operating on autopilot. When I stopped at his destination, I said nothing as he got out.

It was only after I drove away that I was able to breathe and speak again. It wasn't until I went home and lay down for a couple of hours that I had the capacity to report him or even be angry about it.

I was so disappointed in myself! I beat myself up about it for over a year, until one day, I learned about the freeze response. It was as if a lightbulb went off! Finally I understood why I wasn't able to yell or fight like I had promised myself.

The freeze response is automatic and powerful. And as we are about to see, it is also extremely common.

THE FREEZE RESPONSE

Since the 1920s, scientists have been studying and talking about the fight or flight response, two instinctive reactions that all animals have to a threatening or traumatic event. Only in the past two or three decades has it become scientifically accepted that there is a third possibility, known as "tonic immobility," or the freeze response, that is just as common.[36] In fact, in cases of sexual assault it is actually the most common reaction.[37]

When there is a perceived threat to your survival, you will instinctually have one of three responses: fight, flight, or freeze. This happens within 15 milliseconds of perceiving the threat. It's an autonomic response common to all mammals, and it is completely outside a person's conscious control. The amygdala sends signals to the hypothalamus, which releases hormones telling the autonomic nervous system to change the heart rate, breathing, vision, and hearing, and it even thickens the blood and redistributes blood flow. Activity in the prefrontal cortex diminishes and memories formed during this traumatic event will be disjointed and not fully formed. All of this happens before a full second goes by.

For children who are threatened, the response is almost always to freeze, since fight or flight are frequently impossible. People who have experienced the freeze response once are more likely to default to this same response later on. If we were being attacked by predators in the wild, this would be our body's way of protecting us by "playing dead," and it is a natural, instinctual, and intelligent response by our bodies, meant to keep us safe.

The Freeze Response

- Is an autonomic response
- Takes less than 15 milliseconds
- Is a physical survival mechanism
- Is out of your conscious control
- Happens in your brain stem
- Is an evolutionary strategy
- Is meant to keep you alive
- Is not your fault!

Studies have shown that at least 70 percent of sexual assault survivors experience tonic immobility, and it is most common in people who have previously survived childhood or adult sexual assault. There are tragic consequences as a result of the lack of knowledge and understanding about this. Many victims don't understand why they were unable to flee or even speak, and blame themselves for not fighting. Unfortunately, so does much of society, including friends, family members, and many working in the first responder fields and the justice system who have not had adequate trauma training.

Victims who experience tonic immobility are more likely to develop PTSD, blame themselves for the assault, and fail to report it. When they are brave enough to share with others they are often met with statements such as "Why didn't you yell?" or "Why didn't you run?" They are probably already asking themselves the same things. Questions like this compound victim blaming and are never helpful. A helpful statement would be, "You did what you had to do to survive," followed by an explanation of the freeze response.

Crucially, people may cause harm because they mistakenly interpret silence and a lack of movement as passive consent, and are genuinely surprised to find out that the object of their pursuit did not acquiesce but rather was triggered into a freeze response.

This is astonishingly common and is one of the reasons why it is so important to stress that only *enthusiastic* consent is consent.

ENDING VICTIM BLAMING AND SHAMING

We can help shift the culture towards victim support by discussing how the freeze response works and how a lack of understanding about it impacts all of us. It sounds something like this:

WORKSHOP EXERCISE

There is one more thing we need to talk about in order to explain the importance of enthusiastic consent...

Has everyone here heard of the "flight or fight response"?

Give people a chance to respond. If someone brings up the freeze response, congratulate them for guessing what you were about to talk about.

> We now know that there is a third response, the freeze response, that is even more common than the other two responses. Does anyone here know anything about the freeze response?

The freeze response is normal and common.

Allow a short discussion here.

> The freeze response is also known as tonic immobility and it is a result of the body going into survival mode, but seeing no chance of success with fight or flight. For animals in nature it is called "playing dead" and it is the body trying its best to keep itself safe. This is an unconscious reaction made in milliseconds, not a decision. It just happens. And it happens faster than this!

You can snap your fingers to demonstrate.

> People who experience this feel immobilized and disconnected from their bodies. Often, they cannot speak coherently, or even speak at all. During this response, they have trouble forming memories.
>
> People who experience the freeze response can feel confused and ashamed because they don't understand why they were unable to fight or run away. They don't understand that their body had a reaction that was out of their control.
>
> You can help people who've experienced the freeze response by talking about it, recognizing it when you see and hear about it, and not judging people for having this uncontrollable response. If someone tells you about having been unable to speak, or run, or fight, or having fuzzy memories, and not understanding why, you can tell them, "You did what you needed to do to survive." And then you can tell them about the freeze response and how it was not their fault.

ENTHUSIASTIC CONSENT EXERCISES

Unfortunately, because many of us don't understand that this is a natural response to a traumatic event, people may judge themselves or be judged by others. People who are unaware may misinterpret silence and a lack of movement as passive consent. Remember, only ENTHUSIASTIC consent is consent. If you are unsure, ask for and receive an enthusiastic Yes before you do anything. You can have fun with that. Let's do that now.

Can everyone give me their version of an extremely enthusiastic Yes? I'll show you mine.

Do your most theatrical and entertaining version of an enthusiastic Yes. Have fun with it!

Okay, now everyone else.

Get everyone to enthusiastically say yes at the same time.

Substitution for older groups

For older students, you may want to discuss the connection between the freeze response and sexual assault. You could tell them this:

When there is a perceived threat to your survival, you will instinctively have one of three responses: fight, flight or freeze. This happens within 15 milliseconds of perceiving the threat. It's an autonomic response common to all mammals, and it is completely outside a person's conscious control. The amygdala sends signals to the hypothalamus, which releases hormones telling the autonomic nervous system to change your heart rate, breathing, vision, and hearing, and it even thickens your blood and redistributes your blood flow. Activity in your prefrontal cortex diminishes, as well as in other parts of your brain, which messes up your ability to form memories of the event. All this happens before a full second goes by.

Studies show that the freeze response is the most common response to sexual assault, and that once people have experienced the freeze response one time, they are more likely to experience it during future events.

When children are abused by adults they usually have a freeze response, since fighting back or fleeing will often not be options for them. And as these children grow into adults, the freeze response may become their default response. They are also more likely to develop PTSD.

This is why in intimate partner situations it's especially important to get enthusiastic consent. Someone experiencing a freeze response won't be able to give enthusiastic consent, even if they can mumble or murmur.

As the facilitator, you can include the enthusiastic Yes exercise above and/or follow up with some discussion questions that are more mature, such as:

- "How do you know when someone is unenthusiastic with their Yes?"
- "What are some ways you might be able to tell if someone is in a freeze response?"
- "How can you support someone who is blaming themselves for not fighting back?"

SUMMARY

In this chapter, we have talked about the "freeze response," or tonic immobility, what it looks like, and how common it is. We have explained how it plays into a victim self-blaming or being blamed and shamed by others, and how that contributes to very low rates of report for sexual assault. We explain to participants why this is another very important reason to set the bar at enthusiastic consent and do a group exercise in expressing enthusiastic consent.

Chapter 12

Backup, Not Backlash

One of the most powerful transformations that we've experienced as Consent Culture creators is the way the values of collaboration, respect, equity, and bodily autonomy have shifted our views about what should happen when people cause or experience harm. For decades it has been the case that any time anyone with less power speaks up about a consent violation, it is swept under the rug. Even worse, the person who reports, or even just insinuates that something bad is happening, gets backlash for saying something.

It happens when a young woman is chastised to "think of his future." It happens when a boy is shunned for reporting a priest or rabbi's molestation. It happens when a Black child at school is told "It's okay, they didn't mean anything by it." There are countless more examples, but the common response pattern in coercion culture is "hide the problem, then make the person wish they'd never said anything to begin with."

The good news is that slowly, if unevenly, this is shifting. In creating Consent Culture, we have a chance to interrupt these patterns, and find new ways to teach accountability.

MOVING FROM PUNITIVE TO RESTORATIVE JUSTICE

In order to illustrate one of the areas where shifting our approach to justice would make a huge difference for society, we are going to focus on sexual assault in this section.

Most sexual assaults are never reported,[38] and never lead to any kind of resolution, leaving the people who have experienced those violations to suffer in silence. This causes further harm as survivors feel isolated with all the things that they feel unable to say clogging their brains and stewing in their bodies. There are many reasons why people don't talk about these experiences of harm.

First, there is the stigma and shame that is still associated with being a survivor of sexual violence. Often the thought of being seen as a victim, or having to have the conversations that will follow disclosure, will be enough to stop people from speaking out or seeking help.

Second, many victims fear they will not be believed. As with all bullies, perpetrators of sexual violence punch down. Maybe they choose their victims from a lower socio-economic sphere. Maybe they go after someone with a disability. Maybe they choose a victim with an unstable family life. Often the perpetrator will be older, or have more social status or connections to power than the victim. The more marginalized someone is, and the larger the power differential, the less likely they are to be believed if they come forward. When people dig deep to be able to talk about such painful experiences, and then are not believed, it can be extremely damaging.

Third, there is the knowledge that the legal system is often not safe for victims, and that it can re-traumatize people who are already vulnerable. Once a victim of sexual violence reports to the police, they frequently lose their agency over the situation, and often their dignity and humanity are not respected either.[39]

Fourth, often victims know and have compassion for their abusers.[40] They may even love them. They could be dealing with strong feelings of betrayal, and a strong desire for things to go back to how they were before the assault. It can be very enticing to think that perhaps you can forget about it and carry on as if it had never happened. Many victims express that punishment is not their top priority. It's more that they don't want it to happen ever again, to themselves or anyone else.

Lastly, we have all witnessed and understand that most victims who speak up experience societal backlash to some degree. Backlash can be so severe as to cause a survivor of sexual violence to change jobs or careers, leave communities or move geographically, commit suicide,[41] or struggle to ever trust others again.

In Consent Culture, the focus of justice is on helping the victim, getting accountability from the perpetrator, and preventing further harm. This method of harm response is known as restorative justice and it is used in many Indigenous communities.[42] It is also beginning to be used more widely in non-Indigenous communities and on college campuses.[43]

Restorative justice is rooted in the laws and philosophies of some Indigenous nations, as many elements of Consent Culture are. It involves restoring harmony to the whole community. There are three pillars to restorative justice: the needs of the victim, the accountability of the offender, and the engagement of everyone who has been impacted in the justice process.

Everything that occurs is centered on assisting the victim and their family group, through peacemaking circles, victim-offender mediation, and community service and family group conferencing.

Many restorative justice advocates are now promoting transformative justice, a political framework that aims to change the systems and root causes that underlie the violence and trauma that are far too common in the dominant culture. The push for transformative justice has traditionally been, and is still being, spearheaded by grassroots social justice organizations.

Creating Consent Culture is also a part of the transformative justice framework. A culture of coercion is a punitive one, but Consent Culture is about care, prevention, responsibility, and repair. The restorative approach and process bring better accountability and repair to all consent violations, not just for crimes as serious as sexual assault, but also for everyday consent violations that do not rise to the level of criminality. We can even use restorative justice processes with schoolyard disagreements. This is how culture is built.

Talking about restorative and transformative justice can look very different depending on the age of the group. In the workshop, we aim for a straightforward approach that focuses on assisting the victim and the offender taking accountability with a view to preventing the same thing occurring again. (Please find links to restorative and transformative justice websites and books in Appendix 4.)

It is crucial to note that an accountability process is distinct from arbitrary and illogical punishment. A true accountability process may be challenging to undergo, but it is not punitive, and the process is in service of healing and restoration of relationships.

In Consent Culture, an offender will learn that they are expected to take responsibility, be accountable and learn to do better, and apologize meaningfully, and that they will be expected to follow a course which attempts to repair the harm they have caused. And when a victim is supported by society, they will receive backup, not the usual backlash.

CONSENT ACCIDENTS, AND ACCOUNTABILITY

The fact of the matter is that many, if not most, consent violations are accidental, particularly among young people who are still learning to navigate the world. "Accidental," however, does *not* mean trivial. The impact may still be monumental.

Think of a car accident. Sometimes it is the tiniest shift of an angle that makes the difference between walking away shaken but unscathed, or being airlifted to the emergency room.

Often people will say "it was an accident" as an attempt to minimize what happened in a consent violation. But it's the impact on the person who was harmed that matters.

If someone didn't mean to violate consent, their intent is relevant information. Accidents happen, even among people who care about one another. But that it was an accident is only a piece of information, and not a reason to avoid healing and repair.

Sometimes it's not an accident, but it's not exactly malicious either. This is especially true among young people, who are exploring their boundaries and capabilities. Sometimes from the perspective of "I kind of know this is wrong, but I want to see what I can get away with" and sometimes from the perspective of "I don't know what I'm supposed to be doing, but this is kind of like what I've seen modeled, so I'm going to try it and see what happens."

In both cases, this is why addressing consent violations early and often is *crucial* for building Consent Culture. When adults and peers are willing to say "we don't do that here" (whatever "that" is), it helps to establish new norms. We can give guidance to young people who are trying out the coercive ways of interacting they've seen modeled, and support them in taking a step back, assessing, taking responsibility for their actions, and apologizing. We can guide them by listening, collaborating, showing compassion and backing up victims.

EVERYONE MAKES MISTAKES

We all mess up. It's part of being human. From a developmental perspective, young people are still figuring out some foundational pieces of how to interact with others. This is why they need some extra room to make mistakes, without dire or possibly viral consequences, or feeling that there is no way back.

The new term of "canceling" is just another way of saying "shunning," which humanity has been engaged in forever. Ostracism has been a common and deadly form of punishment since time immemorial. Belonging is so crucial that humans will often sacrifice autonomy or dignity to attain it.

If we expect that people can behave better, we need to give them a way to get there. Young people (and older people alike!) can learn to take accountability, apologize, and make restitution. Some people deride calls for accountability as "mob rule" or "cancel culture" and would prefer to go back to sweeping everything under the rug. By providing structure for people to take responsibility, and by appreciating their efforts towards making amends, we can shift this narrative.

Whether a consent violation was acted out intentionally or accidentally doesn't necessarily change the harm to the person who experienced it. They still need the same support, regardless of the intent or age of the perpetrator. We need to back them up.

How can we as adults stand by young people who are experiencing something that is not okay with them? And how can we encourage their peers to do the same? How can we acknowledge that we all, but especially young people, need space to learn these interpersonal skills, without it becoming an environment where the more powerful people get to make mistakes at the expense of the less powerful? Where the more powerful people learn that they are excused when they cause harm, and the less powerful learn that they are expected to tolerate and endure?

In moving away from a dominant culture of coercion, we encounter the problem of *"Who gets to learn and who gets learned on?"*

Building an equitable environment where we can create agreements together requires undermining reflexes like:

- "Boys will be boys."
- "She didn't mean it *like that*."
- "He apologized, so she needs to forgive him."
- "If they were truly Christian, they would forgive."
- "We can't believe just one woman."
- "False accusations are common."

Imagine if we all had more compassion and respect for ourselves and others, practiced asking and hearing each other without shame, and had each other's backs in asserting new norms.

UPSTANDERS, NOT BYSTANDERS

When bullying or harm occurs and we are nearby to witness it, we may not know what to do. In the absence of training or awareness, most people become bystanders.

While research suggests[44] that although many people will intervene when witnessing a violent incident, bystanders often passively watch events unfold, or perhaps even side with a perpetrator. Bystanders might be afraid that they will also be targeted if they intervene on behalf of the victim. They may pretend they don't see what's going on. They may not know what they can do. Bystanders may justify this by convincing themselves that it's none of their business.

As the non-profit organization Hollaback! says, the only thing worse than being targeted, is being targeted while a bunch of people stand around and do nothing about it.[45] Hollaback! is an organization dedicated to fighting harassment—in all its forms. It has a program that trains people on how to stand up to street harassment when they see it happening. The method is called the five Ds of intervention, which stand for:

Distract. Create a distraction to de-escalate the situation. For example, doing things like talking to the target about something unrelated to the harassment, stepping in between them, dropping something, or making a commotion can interrupt and dissuade the harasser.

Delegate. Find someone to help. For example, a security person or other authority figure are options, but also consider asking the person sitting next to you for help. Ask the target if they want the police called before calling the police, because some people don't feel safer with police presence.

Document. Create documentation of the incident. If someone else is already helping the person being harassed, and it's safe to, getting video of the incident can be helpful. But never share that video without the express permission of the person who was harassed.

Delay. After the incident, stay and check in with the person being targeted to see if they are okay and if they need support.

Direct. If it feels safe, directly address the harasser, set a boundary, and name what they are doing. It's best to be short and succinct and not engage in debate. Then, turn your attention to the person being harassed and make sure they are okay.

You can find a link to Hollaback training in Appendix 8.

Hollaback!'s five Ds are great advice when you are present during an incident, but what if you don't hear about something until after it happens? We still have opportunities to support those who have been harmed after the event. They may be seeking support or needing someone to talk to. They may be dealing with others shaming or blaming them for the violation. If so, that is another opportunity to intervene, using these same techniques.

It's also important to intervene with people who harass, by encouraging them to be honest with themselves and others, to apologize, to change their attitudes and behaviors, and to offer repair with whoever they have harmed. This is a powerful way to be an upstander.

We talk about standing up to bullying. Consent violations are an insidious and pervasive type of bullying. Let's teach young people to be upstanders for consent.

OOPS! I MESSED UP! WHAT NOW?

Being able to apologize well and truly strive to make amends are skills that should be universally valued. None of us is completely innocent of harming others, and we can all benefit by becoming better at giving a sincere apology.

As a society, we also need to understand that victims cannot control the amount of time they need to feel better or recover. Expecting and pressuring people to "get over it," forgive, or move on can cause more harm.

In coercion culture, there are two primary outcomes when someone messes up: either acknowledge that it happened and someone gets punished, or else ignore that it ever happened at all. But there is a third possibility in the path of restorative justice.

True accountability is not centered on punishment, but rather on repair. We would argue that a good apology is important for the healing of both the victim and the offender.

In a consent-based culture, *everyone* needs to speak up when something doesn't sit well with them. *Everyone* needs to be capable of hearing feedback about how their actions have impacted others. And *everyone* needs to learn how to apologize and take responsibility for their actions.

THE ANATOMY OF AN APOLOGY

An apology has a purpose, a process, and above all, it should not be a performance!

The purpose of an apology is to communicate to the person harmed that you understand the wrong that you've done and the impact that it has had, that you truly have remorse, and how you are going to behave differently in the future to avoid further harm.

The process begins with recognizing that you have caused harm, either through your own perception, or because you've been told that you have. This should be followed by a period of introspection and self-investigation.

How did you get here? Was there miscommunication or were you misunderstood? Did you speak or act before you thought about the consequences? Did you assume you had permission for something when you did not? Did you simply act selfishly or not have consideration for others?

There are so many questions we can ask ourselves. It's important that we are honest in our reflections. Remember, making a mistake doesn't make *you* a mistake. Doing something wrong is not the same as being wrong for existing! You may feel ashamed for something you've done, and that does not mean that you will feel this way forever.

If you have done an honest reflection and feel that you truly don't have anything to apologize for, then it's better not to give a false apology. The person who was harmed will only sense your insincerity and feel insulted. Apologies need to be heartfelt, or they are worse than useless.

If you realize that you made an error and feel remorse, it's likely that you will then want to make amends and make changes so that you don't hurt others again. Next, think through what changes you need to make to avoid further harm. How will you change your behavior so that you don't end up here again?

Once you have that all figured out, you are ready to apologize!

There are four parts to a meaningful apology:

1. **Actually say you're sorry.** Use the words "sorry" or "apologize."

2. **Describe what you are sorry for.** Be specific and comprehensive so that others can see that you have really thought it through and truly understand what you have done wrong. Not "I'm sorry I hurt your feelings" but something more specific like, "I'm sorry I called you a stupid-butt after you told me to stop it."

3. **Name the impact or effect your actions have had.** Make it clear that you understand how your actions have affected the other person. You don't have to get it perfect, but a meaningful apology includes this step. It can be painful to describe, but sharing this helps the other person see that you are taking responsibility and that you're empathetic to how they feel.

4. **Share how you're going to behave differently moving forward.** This shows that you won't cause this same harm again.

WATCH YOUR STEP!

There are some pitfalls to watch out for when apologizing.

Some people say sorry and then insist that you accept their apology because they said they were sorry already! But this skips the whole process required to make a proper apology and is basically an attempt to quickly bypass the discomfort of the moment.

Other people avoid taking real responsibility by centering themselves as the person suffering. They cry and tear at their clothes, bang their head against the wall and yell about how they are worthless, no good people who don't deserve your forgiveness. This practically requires the person who was harmed to come to their rescue and reassure them that all is forgiven.

Then there is the infamous non-apology apology, often given by politicians and celebrities:

- "I'm sorry you felt that way."

- "I'm sorry you thought that this thing happened."

- "I'm sorry *if* I caused harm, but I categorically deny the accusation."

These aren't real apologies, and there is no point. Just stop.

Another positive outcome of learning to apologize is that it aids your own personal growth. Growth depends on getting out of your comfort zone and learning new skills. Let's support one another to practice these skills, and create more ease around taking accountability and making amends as a regular part of our day-to-day lives.

WORKSHOP EXERCISE

So how do you talk to your participants about being an upstander and apologizing? It goes something like this:

> Let's talk about when we mess up, because none of us is perfect, and we all make mistakes and hurt other people, even when we don't mean to. In Consent Culture, when someone is hurt, we focus on supporting the person in pain, and prioritize what they need to feel supported. The person who did the hurting is expected to be accountable and make amends. This can feel scary at first, because maybe you've taken responsibility for something before and then been punished. But that's not how we do things in Consent Culture.
>
> Has anyone heard of restorative justice?

Give a moment for answers.

> Right now, we have a punitive justice system, but many Indigenous peoples have traditionally used a system of restorative justice, and it's having a resurgence of popularity now. It's called restorative justice because rather than focusing on punishing wrongdoing, it focuses on restoring harmony to a community.
>
> In a restorative justice system, everyone in the community engages by standing up to bad behavior, supporting people who've been targeted, and encouraging those who have harmed others to apologize and make amends.
>
> Let's talk about an example. If one of you was to film yourself calling a classmate names until they cried, and then shared that video online, what do you think would normally happen?

Get some answers. Keep asking questions until you get the full picture of what would happen to the student who did the harassing, the student who was harassed, and how it might impact both students' family members or classmates. For instance, if the one harassing were suspended, would the victim feel safer when the harasser returned to school?

> Now, if we were in this restorative system that meets the needs of the person harmed, and strives to restore harmony to everyone involved, what do you think would happen?

Again, keep asking questions and gently guiding the conversation until the participants can get a general picture of the harassed student being supported, the student who did the harassing taking accountability, the root causes of the action being explored, and everyone coming out of it feeling better understood and that it won't happen again.

You could ask questions like:

> — "What do you think the difference is between accountability and punishment?"
> — "How can we back up the person who has been harmed?"
> — "How can we support the person who did the harm to take accountability?"
> — "What actions or words would help you feel more confident that this wouldn't happen again?"

> Let's talk about harassment. We all know what it's like to be a bystander when someone is being harassed or bullied, and many of us know the pain of being targeted while people stand by and watch. Let's not stand by, let's stand up when we see someone targeting someone else. In Consent Culture, we are upstanders, not bystanders.
>
> What do you think some examples of being an upstander might look like?

You can get a few examples and perhaps add a few yourself, such as:

• Getting help when someone is being harassed.

• Intervening if you feel safe to.

• Trying to distract the person who is doing the harassing so that the person being targeted can get away.

In Consent Culture, we want to be good at apologizing when we've hurt someone. By being good at it, I don't mean putting on a good show. Let's learn what is involved in apologizing well and practice it.

I'm going to apologize to the group now, and I want you to grade me. I'm really sorry if something I did made you feel bad.

How was that? Do you feel like my apology was sincere?

Get some feedback from the group before you try again.

Okay, how's this. I'm really sorry that I made you do some weird exercises. I know that it made you feel embarrassed, and I didn't want to make you feel that way.

How was that? Was it better when I was more specific about what I did wrong and how it made you feel? How could we make it better?

Okay, one last try. I'm really sorry that I made you do some weird exercises. I know that it made you feel embarrassed, and I don't want you to feel that way. I'm going to try really hard not to make you do any more weird exercises.

How was that? Was it better that I said how I was going to change my behavior so that I wouldn't do it again?

Deliver this line for comedic effect.

Just to be clear, that was all for practice, and I am definitely going to have you do more weird exercises!

— "Any 'aha!' moments from this demonstration?"
— "Will you apologize differently after this? Why, or why not?"

OPTIONAL DISCUSSION TOPIC

If you have time, go to Hollaback!'s website and use one of its exercises to have the participants explore and practice the five Ds of effective bystander intervention. Afterwards, have a discussion about how these five Ds can be used in other circumstances besides someone being harassed on the street. Some discussion questions might be:

- Which of the five Ds do you think you might try? Why?

- What do you think are some good ways to de-escalate a situation?

- When do you think it's okay to document someone being targeted?

- What are some good ways to check in with someone after an incident?

SUMMARY

To recap, in this chapter we have gone over the differences between a punitive and a restorative justice system, how "canceling" people doesn't lead to accountability, and how to be an upstander rather than a bystander. We also talked about what to do when we're the one who has messed up and how to give a meaningful apology.

Chapter 13

Taking it Online

Online culture is often a knock-down, drag-out land of sneering confrontation. On top of that we have to take all kinds of precautions to avoid online predators, and protect our private information.

But what if we could actually make these virtual landscapes kinder, more compassionate and safer for everyone?

The tools for respecting personal autonomy throughout this book are transferable to online interactions. The ability to say and hear no, and collaborate to find a mutually agreeable way to interact online comes from these same principles. Defaulting to No when you're unsure, pausing to notice what you really want, listening for an enthusiastic Yes—all of these remain the same online.

However, there are some aspects to online interactions that make knowing and expressing our boundaries more challenging. Being one step removed from an interaction can lead to reduced empathy,[46] reckless statements, and painful regret. So, let's explore what we can do to avoid the pitfalls of virtual interaction, and deliberately create Consent Culture online.

ERICA
Can I take it back?

I have more than a few personal stories of oversharing online, or being inspired by a quick burst of anger or passion to say things that were hurtful to others, leading to many hours of regretful anguish. And I'm not talking about the distant past or even last year. This is an ongoing challenge for me, and maybe for you too.

It's not like I've never messed up in a real-life conversation. I have often been told I have "foot in mouth" disease. But in person it seems easier to address what I've said and mend things in the moment. I cringe when I think about the harmful things I've said online reverberating throughout the web.

That's why I've started using the "Why am I sharing this?" exercise that comes a little later in this chapter. It's a great tool to remind myself to pause and think, before I step in it!

MAKING VIRTUAL SPACE A BETTER PLACE

Online, when we feel strongly about a topic, or we are triggered by another's comment, it can feel safe and easy to go on blast mode. Perhaps we are just having a bad day and the consequences of being mean to someone we vehemently disagree with seem unimportant. But the consequences are real, and it causes real pain every day.

We can apologize, we can learn and grow from the feedback we receive, and we can evolve, but it is very hard to take back what we've said online. That's why we encourage people of all ages to use the following tools to contribute to a culture of consent.

Embodied check-ins

In Chapter 7, we went through some techniques of feeling into the body to determine if we are a Yes or a No to something.

Embodied check-ins are about turning our attention to our bodily cues and listening for information (e.g. tense stomach, hunched shoulders) in order to understand how we really feel about what is happening.

When an interaction online feels uncomfortable, take some deep breaths and pause to get in touch with the what and why of your bodily sensations. Noticing what you feel, and what you actually want or don't want, can help you to decide how to engage (*or not*) in an online interaction.

Why am I sharing this?

Here is a practice that both Marcia and Erica do versions of before posting online.

Develop a habit of asking yourself why, before each online share.

Perhaps you want to have a checklist of criteria that a post needs to meet before it can be shared. You could choose a handful of these questions:

- Is this true?

- Is this kind?

- Is this necessary?

- Who is this serving?

- Will this be helpful information for someone?

- Will this reflect well on me?

- Will this make me, or someone else, happier?

Only you can decide what the criteria for posting or responding are for you, but setting a standard for your interactions will help you make better choices.

Once you've done this, give yourself some kind of memory aid in order to remember to ask yourself the questions you've chosen, such as a note on your computer or a sticker on your phone.

Upstander versus bystander

We've talked before about the difference between being an upstander and being a bystander. If we want to create a virtual culture of consent, then we need to intervene if we see someone being targeted or victimized online.

We can do more than just not taking part in abuse. We can respond publicly in a thread. We can take people aside privately or in their direct messages and talk about how they are hurting someone. And, most importantly, we can check in with and support those being targeted.

De-escalation skills

When conflict arises online it is so easy for things to escalate quickly. We can use the tools we've already discussed to bring the temperature down. One of the benefits of interacting online is that we can take a break before getting back to someone.

De-escalation looks like going offline and re-evaluating what is happening. Online communication lacks tone of voice and body language cues, so it's especially important to double-check that what we have understood is what was intended.

If possible, shifting the communication offline can help with de-escalation. A simple phone call or video chat can cool things down considerably.

Did they ask for advice?

Sometimes offering advice to someone online feels like the friendly option. Perhaps you've been through something that the other person is currently struggling with, and you want to encourage them, or let them know that they are not alone.

But other times giving advice can be a way to assert a sense of superiority, reassure oneself of being a savior, or even to criticize in a back handed way.

So, how do you make sure that you are offering advice for the right reasons? Or if you should offer it at all? And what do you do when others offer you unwanted advice and it makes you uncomfortable or angry?

One thing you can do is ask, "Do you want advice, someone to listen to you, or something else?" Or ask if there is a way that you can help.

And what if someone gives *you* online advice that you didn't ask for, and it feels bad to you? As we discussed before, when triggered online you have the unique opportunity to take a breather, take your time, check in with your feelings, and respond when you have a clear mind.

At that point, you can consider if the person meant well, or if it was passive-aggressive behavior, or perhaps if it was an outright attack. No matter what their intent was, one way to deflect it is to let them know that you appreciate them trying to help you, but going forward you would prefer for them to ask you first whether you're looking for advice.

ONLINE BOUNDARIES, "SHARENTING," AND IMAGES

A big part of consent in today's world has to do with digital consent. Digital consent encompasses respecting other people's right to their online privacy, respecting other people's right to freely communicate with others online, and respecting others' choices to either share or not share images of themselves. Knowing and communicating our boundaries, and respecting the boundaries of others, is just as important online as it is offline.

One controversial consent issue online is the very common practice of "sharenting." The term was coined in 2012 by Erin McKean in the *Wall Street Journal*,[47] and describes the sharing or over-sharing of children's photos, videos, and information online by their parents, without the child's consent. This can have life-long consequences that parents frequently don't take into consideration.[48]

In a world in which obtaining personal data has become an extremely profitable industry, and the structure of this new economy is being described as surveillance capitalism,[49] there is a lot to consider about a child's inability to consent to sharing their images and information.

Beyond the issues of parents introducing their children to a virtual world, there are the very real consequences of making them vulnerable to online predators, identity fraud, facial identification, bullying, a skewed sense of self, and unforeseeable outcomes due to future developments in technology. All of this at an age when they are unable to understand the ramifications of their information being shared or meaningfully agree to it.

Meanwhile, friends and family may be clamoring for more pictures.

We bring up sharenting to highlight the complications of sharing images and information online. Most of us can relate to the dilemma of having innocent intentions that lead to potentially dire outcomes.

When the intentions are not well meaning, it can become downright terrorizing. Sharing unflattering images is a common form of bullying. Revenge porn and indiscriminate sharing of sexual images can ruin lives. The non-consensual sharing of photos, particularly nude or sexual ones, takes us into the arena of criminality and the law once again. Just as pressuring, threatening, or coercing someone into doing sexual acts is sexual violence and a crime, it is also sexual violence to coerce or guilt someone into sharing explicit photos or video.

Unfortunately, the victims of non-consensual photo sharing are often unsupported, and they can suffer from victim shaming and devastating harassment. A common outcome is for victims to feel that they must change schools, or even towns, to escape the abuse, and many develop depression, anxiety, or other mental health issues.[50]

A good rule of thumb is: "Without consent, it's not sent."

There are no easy answers here. This is a great topic for discussion, and we have suggested some questions that you can share with participants in the optional discussion section.

Sharing these tools for creating virtual Consent Culture is something we do in the workshop, and it sounds something like this:

WORKSHOP DISCUSSION/EXERCISE

Creating Consent Culture is something we can do online as well as in real life. Let's look at the tools we've already learned, and how they apply to our online interactions.

Practicing saying and hearing no, thanking others for expressing clear boundaries, and checking in with ourselves to know what we want and don't want are important skills for interacting online.

Defaulting to a No when we are a Maybe, being clear communicators, and being an upstander rather than a bystander are all great ways to contribute to a better culture online.

Let's do a quick brainstorm. Let's break into our groups of three and take a minute to talk about some of the challenges of communicating online. See if you can come up with a few ways that online interactions can be hard. Please get into your groups and do that now.

After a minute or two, stop the discussion and ask the group for a few examples that they've come up with.

Clearly some things are different online, and there are a few extra tools that can help us with those added challenges. One thing that happens online is that people feel removed from the interaction and are likely to show less empathy. People tend to say things online that they wouldn't say in person and conflicts can arise and escalate quickly. Sometimes there are misunderstandings because we can't hear the person's tone of voice or see their body language.

Those are some of the challenges, but one of the benefits of online interactions is that we can step away from our devices and check in with ourselves. Then we can either decide not to take part anymore, or else come back when we are calm and clear about what we need to say.

We've all said things online that we regret, and if we can keep in mind that it is harder to take things back once they are out there on the internet, perhaps we can make better choices about what we share.

The next time you have an interaction online that is upsetting you, try taking a break and using the embodied check-in before going back to the conversation. Maybe you'll decide you don't want to go back to that conversation at all!

I'm going to show you a tool that's called, "Why am I sharing this?" Let's pull out a sheet of paper and put together a checklist of things to think about before you share or post. They can include, "Is this a kind thing to say?", "Is this helpful?" or, "Is this really true?".

Does anyone want to share any of their pre-posting conditions?

Give a moment for discussion.

When you have a list of considerations that you like, you could put a little sticker on your phone to remind yourself to go over that checklist before hitting "post" or "send." Maybe you want to challenge yourself to do this every time for a couple of weeks and see if you can turn it into a habit.

We can also be upstanders rather than bystanders online, and intervene when we see someone being targeted. For example, we can respond publicly in a thread. We can take people aside privately or in their direct messages and talk about how they are hurting someone. And, most importantly, we can check in with and support those being targeted.

What other ideas do you have for how to be an upstander online?

Give a moment for discussion.

Let's keep in mind that being online has been shown to decrease our ability to be empathetic, so we need extra time to step back and make sure we're bringing the same amount of empathy and compassion to our virtual encounters as we do in person. That's a challenge for everyone!

Finally, why not pause before we give advice online, and ask ourselves, "Did they ask for advice?" We might think that we have the perfect words of wisdom, because we've been through that experience before. One way to bring Consent Culture to the internet is to ask "Do you want advice, someone to listen to you, or something else?" Or ask if there is a way that you can help.

If you are given advice that you didn't ask for, and it's upsetting, take a deep breath and remind people that you would like to be asked if you want advice before it is offered.

OPTIONAL DISCUSSION TOPIC

There are more questions about digital consent than there are answers, and this makes for an opportunity to have powerful discussions. You can lead a discussion with participants by asking questions such as:

- When is it okay, or not okay, to share friends' or relatives' pictures online? Should you always ask for permission? Why, or why not?

- How do you feel when someone shares your picture, or a video, without asking? Is it different if it's your parents or older relatives who do it?

- What does it mean if someone other than a parent demands to have your passwords?

- How can we ask others to respect our boundaries around sharing online?

- Do you have other ideas for how to be kind and respectful online that we haven't already talked about?

(There are resources to help with issues of online consent in Appendix 8.)

SUMMARY

In this chapter, we've looked at some of the unique challenges of creating Consent Culture online. We have talked about how it's easy to feel less empathy and have more misunderstandings in digital interactions, and some tools we can use to counteract this. We've touched on the evolving ethical questions about sharing images online, both innocently and with bad intent, and we have talked about the temptation to give unsolicited advice online.

Chapter 14

When Is the Hug Over?

MARCIA

In 2008, after nearly a decade in New York, I moved to San Francisco. I was ready for a change of scenery, more access to nature, and less terrible winters. I was eager to live in a place with more open space and excited to meet colleagues I'd only known online. After growing up in the slow-moving South, and spending my young adulthood racing non-stop through the Big Apple, I was excited for life to move at a medium speed. By then, I had spent the previous four years cuddling with strangers and talking about the nuances of touch and consent with loads of major media outlets. I was ready to take on the West Coast.

But in no way was I ready for this: "The California Yummy Hug."

The California Yummy Hug is a term my friends used to describe the way that, in certain personal growth, festival and new-age subcultures, some people will greet you with a hug.

Okay, fine, I was comfortable with hugging, but there was more. They would then rub my back, breathe in deeply, and then let out an audible "MMmmMMmmmmmMMmmmmmm"—and somehow *never* get the hint when I was done. They'd hold on, always a few beats too long, and *then*, as if that weren't enough, as they pulled away, grab my shoulders with both hands, look me in the eyes and slowly nod their head, as though we had just shared something meaningful together.

But nearly every time, it wasn't meaningful to me. It felt, at various times, weird, performative, or just grabby.

I could see that some of this was a cultural difference, as we talked about in Chapter 9. And I could tell that some people were genuinely trying to make our connection more intimate.

The problem was that it was more intimate than I wanted it to be.

Over time, I found ways to be more assertive with ending a Yummy Hug. I would step back as the inhale began, and either hold their hands to keep a short distance between us (when I wanted to maintain connection without the moaning), or put my hands in a prayer position in front of me (another California affectation). Sometimes I would use words to intentionally create a tone shift, stepping away as I said brightly, "Cool! Nice to see you!"

Learning how to end an encounter, both verbally and non-verbally, is a skill that has served me well—especially since I plan on staying in California!

ENDING AN INTERACTION IS DIFFERENT THAN BEGINNING ONE

Many of us have had the experience of being in a consensual interaction that we are ready to have end, and yet it goes on. It might be a hug, a conversation, a cuddle, a handshake or a sexual encounter. You try to pull away, but the other person is not picking up on your cues.

While beginning an interaction requires the consent of everyone involved, ending an interaction should happen when any person involved is ready to stop.

During this last part of the workshop, you'll be leading the participants to practice closing an interaction. What do you do when the other person is not picking up on your cues that you aren't into it anymore? And how can we avoid being the oblivious squeezer?

After going over how to consensually end an interaction, we'll lead one more group exercise in order to practice everything we've learned in the workshop. And finally, we'll give one last demonstration, this time on what to do when you have to deal with people who have not taken the workshop.

A consensual interaction is over when anyone in it is done.

WORKSHOP EXERCISE

First let's start with how to end an interaction, and it sounds something like this:

> This brings us to our final question: When is the hug over? Consent is given from moment to moment and in Consent Culture you are encouraged to change your mind at any time. When a handshake, a hug, or any physical interaction is consensual, it should end when one person decides they are done. We usually rely on body language to understand when this is, but that's not always clear, and some people are better at reading body language than others.
>
> Let's find a partner and pick an A and a B for one last greeting. Actually, two greetings. This works best with either a handshake or a hug, so if that doesn't appeal to you just sit it out.
>
> Decide together if you're going to do a handshake or a hug for this exercise. Then, shake hands or hug your partner and A you will be the one to stop first. B, try to get as close as you can to noticing exactly when A decides to stop. Once you've done that, trade places and do it again. Really try to see if you can pinpoint the exact moment the other person wants to stop.

If someone is not picking up on your cues, use your words. You can say, "Thank you, I'm done now." Or, "That was nice, let's stop now."

Does anyone have any "aha!" moments or anything that they would like to share from this greeting exercise?

We are nearing the end of the workshop now, and I'd like us to practice a few of the skills we've learned so far. I'm going to ask you to walk around the room and ask for handshakes, or hugs, or fist bumps, or high fives, or a wave, and this time if you are a Yes you can say yes and do those things. But you have to say no at least every other time. In other words, if you said yes this time, say no the next time, even if you would like to say yes.

You can also spend the whole exercise practicing your No. Remember to thank your partners when they say no.

Let this go on for a few minutes. Play it by ear.

Thanks everyone. We've practiced saying and hearing yes and no and how to check in with ourselves to know whether we are a Yes or a No. We've talked about changing our minds and checking in with our partners. We've learned different ways to collaborate for a mutually agreeable interaction and practiced knowing when the interaction is over.

OPTIONAL DISCUSSION TOPIC

If you have time, you could tell this story that includes some of the concepts we've been exploring with the group, and discuss the follow-up questions (or come up with your own):

Anna has a hard time saying no to her friends, so she will often find herself doing the things that they want to do and talking about the things that they want to talk about. That wouldn't be so bad, except that she finds herself listening to one of her friends talk endlessly when she would rather be doing something else. Or playing a game with another friend who never seems to stop, even when they have been playing for hours. She is so worried about getting sucked into a long game or conversation that she has started avoiding her friends.

- What could Anna do differently?

- What do you remember about what we learned earlier about changing your mind?

- How could Anna let her friends know when she is done?

- What could Anna's friends do differently to help Anna feel more confident to speak up?

SUMMARY

In this chapter, we have been over how to consensually end an interaction and lead participants through a few exercises to practice reading body language and communicating when the interaction is over. Finally, we had one last greeting exercise to practice several of the tools that have been learned throughout the workshop.

Chapter 15

Practice, Practice, Practice

In this book, we have outlined the basics of building Consent Culture. We have talked about the skills involved: Saying yes and no, what to do with a Maybe, how to ask for what you want, changing your mind, looking for the enthusiastic Yes, listening well, de-escalation and intervention techniques, reading body language, and apologizing well.

We have also talked about the shifts in attitude that underlie Consent Culture: respect for bodily autonomy, understanding power and privilege, and collaboration rather than permission-seeking or gatekeeping. We have reviewed the freeze response and some of the ways it is misunderstood. We've talked about how the law is the absolute bare minimum and that Consent Culture is about how to treat one another with respect and how to find what is mutually agreeable and fun.

As workshop facilitators, we have witnessed many participants have major epiphanies and make substantial changes in their lives as a result of experiencing a few hours in a consent-based social context. We also know, from follow-up conversations, that it takes practice to truly internalize a consent-based approach to the world—one where we each expect our own bodily autonomy to be respected, we each respect others, and we work together to find mutually agreeable interactions as often as possible.

MARCIA

Learning consent is not "one and done"
Even after nearly 20 years of facilitating Cuddle Party events, teaching consent in my classes, supporting individuals in their

repair processes, and consulting for community building and incident response, I'm still learning about nuances of consent, and finding things to unlearn.

There are times I still railroad over another person because I want to believe what they are saying isn't important or doesn't apply to me. There are still times when I'm flummoxed by a stranger who feels entitled to crowd my space or make comments about my body. As a white person, I'm still in a deep, life-long unlearning process around the ways I've been taught to disregard and dismiss the words, experiences, and bodies of people of color. As a woman, I still have to navigate the sometimes shocking and sometimes terrifying ways that some men casually dehumanize or sexualize me and other women. As a child of a chronically ill parent, I am still acutely attuned to some forms of disability, while I catch myself being wildly oblivious to others. As a user of the internet, I'm still tempted to jump into the fray to be "on the right side" when some juicy drama is going down. As a workshop facilitator, I have to remember to slow down when I get pushback on something that seems obvious and foundational to me.

Learning about consent helps give me skills to do this, and solid ground to return to when I feel defensive, angry, dismissed, or demoralized.

It's not about taking a consent class and saying pass/fail. It's about how we practice these skills in our lives. You don't have to become a consent expert or even have the correct words. You just have to choose to live, as much as possible, from a place of respect, curiosity about other people, and a willingness to figure it out together.

ERICA

Over and over again

Regardless of how much self-work I've done, I find myself in situations where the boundaries are unfamiliar or more complex than those I have already gotten better at. I struggle to find my balance and to use the tools that I practice and share. Sometimes

I only realize afterwards what I really wanted to do with someone. Often I find it difficult to express the anger or frustration that I'm feeling when my boundaries are crossed. I still don't always feel safe enough to do that.

To this day, I can catch myself giggling when I am actually nervous or frustrated. Or freezing when I wish I was yelling. Or saying something I know to be true as if I were asking a question, because apparently my unconscious thinks that will keep me safer? (Yes, I did that on purpose.) I find myself in the surreal position of listening to words or laughter emerging from my own vocal chords while my brain reels and asks, "WTF is this coming out of my mouth right now?!"

On the flip side, I also catch myself making the assumption that everyone loves hugs as much as I do, even though I now know very well this isn't always true. Or not fully respecting the personal boundaries of my adult daughter, because it is such a habit.

Then begins the process of going over it, figuring out what I could have done better, what I should have said. Wondering if I'll ever be able to get this right the first time. Realizing that I may not. That these things may always happen. That next time I may again go in for the hug before realizing that the other person's body language is not enthusiastic and that I should have asked first. Or that I may freeze again when I feel threatened, no matter how many times I've told myself that I will yell and I will fight.

Luckily for me, one of the greatest things to come out of my mid-life health crisis has been the gift of self-compassion. It totally transformed my life. Another realization that came as a shock to me (and may come as a shock to you as well), was that life does not actually require us to judge ourselves harshly and flog ourselves repeatedly. If you are lucky enough to have never had this particular challenge, please believe me that many of your participants will be struggling with it. It is so important to remind them to have compassion for themselves if they don't get this right on the first, or second, or twentieth try. We all have to keep practicing.

CHANGING CULTURE IS HARD,
BUT DOABLE (AND FUN!)

As you carry on the work as a Consent Culture creator, both as a facilitator for others, and in your own life, it may feel like a lot of work at times. It's true that grappling with the impact of coercion, oppression, rape culture, and trauma is heavy work. But working towards a consent-based world is ultimately joyful work. You can't undo all of the terrible things that happen in the world, but you can create pockets of safety, comfort, and play for yourself and the people in your life. These pockets may be small at first, but we know from experience that they are inherently appealing to many people, and they can grow quickly.

Change doesn't happen in a vacuum. As a facilitator, you have a terrific opportunity to create experiences that your participants can learn from and carry forward in their own lives. As a leader, you have a chance to be the one to say, "This is how we do things here." As a member of your school or work community, you have an opportunity to stand up for others being treated well. In your personal life, you can adjust your friendships and partnerships to include more checking in, more listening and more collaboration. As you put these practices into action, you will see change ripple around you.

Be mindful of the tendency to think in binary and punitive terms about consent. Respect and collaboration are on a spectrum, and we are all on a learning curve. Even when we are trying to be conscientious, we will still step on one another's toes and jostle each other at times. When consent incidents happen, remember that it's about lessening the impact on the person who is harmed and shortening the turn-around time towards meaningful repair.

It will serve you well to have compassion for yourself and others in the process. Forgive yourself for the things you didn't know and couldn't have done better. Learn from others. Stay curious and open to new information. Recognize that you'll have bad days when you're under-resourced or emotionally triggered. Apologize for your mistakes earnestly, and don't carry them around as weapons to bludgeon yourself with. Extend this grace to others who are trying to do better as well, to the degree that you are able.

But most of all, have fun with it! The old culture of coercion is creepy, cruel, and fundamentally unfair. The new culture of consent is filled with courage, joy, and possibilities we haven't even begun to imagine yet.

PUTTING COMPASSION INTO PRACTICE

Just as Consent Culture is about having respect for ourselves and others, it is also about having compassion for ourselves and others. Help your participants to truly find compassion for their own struggles with the human condition. It sounds something like this:

WORKSHOP EXERCISE

Learning Consent Culture and unlearning all the stuff that makes it harder takes practice. You may not get this right the first time, or the second time, or the twentieth time, and that's okay. Keep practicing and it will become clearer each time. You will get better at it. You may have days when you think, "I could have done that better," or, "I wish I had listened more closely," or, "I should have kicked their ass!" but please don't be hard on yourself. This does not come automatically to anyone and we all need to practice. If you don't know how to be kind to yourself, close your eyes and think of someone that you love very much. Now, imagine treating yourself the same way you would treat them.

Another thing to remember is that sometimes there are situations where it is not safe to say no or state your boundaries, no matter how much you want to. That is not the time to practice! If you find yourself in a situation like that, trust your instincts, and do and say whatever it takes to stay safe and extract yourself from that dangerous situation. Ask for help from someone you trust afterwards.

We are coming to the end of the workshop and we will have time for questions and a discussion. You can see me afterwards if you have questions. Now there is just one more demonstration.

At this point if you don't have an assistant, ask if one of the participants is willing to come up and violate your boundaries for the demonstration. This usually gets a laugh.

Okay, you know how to have consensual interactions now, but what about when you go out in the world and run into people who don't? I'm going to demonstrate a few ways to handle people crossing your boundaries.

If you do have an assistant, ask them to come up and when they are standing beside you ask them to violate your boundaries. You could ask them to touch your arm or hug you without asking, if you are both comfortable with that.

The first time they violate your boundaries, pull back and say, "Oh, I need to be asked for touch."

The second time, move their hand away or step back and say, "Not cool."

The third time, pull away and say, "I didn't hear you ask me if I wanted to do that—have you heard of Consent Culture?"

Thank your assistant/participant for helping in the demonstration. Turn to the group.

> Congratulations everyone! You've completed the workshop and you are now certified Consent Culture creators. Thank you for helping to create Consent Culture.

Hand out certificates of completion if you have them. We have provided an example of a participant completion form with main points to remember along with a link to a more colorful version in Appendix 5.

If you have time take questions and mediate a discussion of "aha!" moments from the workshop.

Possible questions:

> – "Does anyone have any 'aha!' moments from the workshop that they would like to share?"
> – "What do you feel is the most important thing you learned over the last few hours?"
> – "What is one thing you will do differently after taking this workshop?"

SUMMARY

To recap, we have gone over the need to keep practicing the tools we have learned, and to have compassion for ourselves and others if we don't get it right away. We have demonstrated what to do when people don't seek our consent, and we have summarized what participants have covered throughout the workshop. We have also congratulated the participants for completing the workshop, and handed out certificates.

Building a Consent-Oriented World

We would love to have more Consent Culture Intro facilitators!

If you are going to facilitate some or all of these exercises and would like more instruction or to see how it can look in real life, there is an online course available.

To find out more about the online course or to learn more about becoming a certified facilitator, please visit Erica at her website www.creatingconsentculture.com.

We will now list some resources to bolster your facilitation skills.

FACILITATION

Cuddle Party has a virtual and online training to help you facilitate powerful, fulfilling group experiences: http://cuddleparty.com

Values Question Protocol: A video to help educators investigate their own values bias: www.youtube.com/watch?v=22qmE7wDYIk

TRAUMA-INFORMED EDUCATION

Educational websites about being trauma informed:

- www.ascd.org/publications/educational_leadership/oct19/vol77/num02/Trauma-Informed_Teaching_Strategies.aspx

- https://safesupportivelearning.ed.gov/trauma-sensitive
  -schools-training-package

Trauma-informed sex and consent education: https://sparked.net

MANDATED REPORTING
Explanations about mandatory reporting in the US:

- https://usagym.org/pages/education/safesport/pdfs/fedreport-
  ing.pdf

- www.childwelfare.gov/pubPDFs/manda.pdf

Frequently asked questions about mandated reporting: www.d2l.org/
wp-content/uploads/2017/01/Mandated_Reporting_07.07.15.pdf

LAND ACKNOWLEDGEMENT
Resources to help you with giving a meaningful land acknowledgement:

- Guidebook to indigenous protocol: www.ictinc.ca/guidebook-to
  -indigenous-protocol

- A US-based movement to honor Native Land: https://usdac.us/
  nativeland

- Native Land Digital has maps and information about Indigenous
  Nations: https://native-land.ca

- A guide to Indigenous land acknowledgements: https://nativegov.
  org/a-guide-to-indigenous-land-acknowledgment

PRONOUNS
Resources about using correct pronouns:

- www.adl.org/education/resources/tools-and-strategies/lets-get
  -it-right-using-correct-pronouns-and-names

- https://lgbt.ucsf.edu/pronounsmatter

- https://lgbtlifecenter.org/pronouns

Partnering During the Workshop

Some participants may find self-directed pairing to be challenging. Asking young people to put themselves into pairs or groups can create an instant popularity contest which can be devastating for the kids who are already losing that battle every day. This happens with adult participants as well.

Here are some ways you can make partnering easier:

- If seated, have them turn to the person next to them.

- Line them up in two rows, facing each other, and they then pair off with the person across the row.

- Select the pairs and groups yourself and designate the participants as As and Bs.

- Hand out a bunch of objects that match each other and have them find the person who has the matching object. This can be something as simple as differently colored popsicle sticks.

- Use an app—there are a variety of apps that teachers use to group students, such as Random Student Generator, Class Dojo, Random Group Maker, and the Team Shake app.

As we've mentioned, sitting out is also an option.

Generating Group Agreements

What better way to model the principles of consent in action than by creating agreements for your workshop together? If appropriate, you can ask your students what agreements would help them to feel comfortable and confident to participate, and see what you all can come up with together.

Some examples of group agreements include:

- **Listen with curiosity.** We won't make assumptions about other people's values, lifestyles, identities, behaviors, or feelings. We will stay open and curious to hear how others experience things.

- **Ask questions.** We are encouraged to ask questions and they are valued by the facilitator. However, we do not ask personal or embarrassing questions.

- **Adopt a non-judgmental approach.** It's okay to disagree with others, but we will not shame, judge, or make fun of them. We agree to challenge the opinion, not the person.

- **Take space/make space.** Those of us who like to talk in groups will challenge ourselves to wait before speaking. Those of us who tend to hold back will challenge ourselves to speak up.

- **What's said here, stays here. What's learned here, leaves here.** We agree to share what we've learned, but not other people's stories or identities.

- **Tell my own story.** We will use "I" statements, and avoid making generalizations about groups. We will discuss examples but not use other people's names or descriptions in a way that identifies them.

- **When one person is talking, others are listening.** We agree not to talk over one another and to avoid cross-talk.

Legal Information

SEXUAL ASSAULT AND SEXUAL HARASSMENT

It's a great idea to look at what the laws are with groups who are mature enough to benefit from this. We have often been shocked at how little public knowledge there is about the definitions of assault and harassment.

Here are general descriptions of sexual assault and sexual harassment that you can share with your participants,

Sexual harassment

Sexual harassment laws were designed to protect people in schools and in the workplace from harassment. Sexual harassment is generally defined as unwelcome sexual advances, requests for sexual favors, and other verbal or physical conduct of a sexual nature when submission to or rejection of this conduct explicitly or implicitly affects an individual's employment, unreasonably interferes with an individual's work performance, or creates an intimidating, hostile or offensive work/school environment.

Sexual assault

This involves touching someone else sexually against their will without their explicit consent. It is up to the person seeking the sexual touching to determine if there is explicit consent; and being intoxicated or assuming that silence is consent are not legal defenses. People who are intoxicated, unconscious, or underage cannot legally give consent.

The exact definitions vary from state to state and from country to country, so do the research for your region. Here are some resources that will point you in the right direction:

- https://apps.rainn.org/policy

- www.equalrights.org/issue/economic-workplace-equality/sexual-harassment

- https://canadianwomen.org/the-facts/sexual-assault-harassment

RESTORATIVE AND TRANSFORMATIONAL JUSTICE

More and more communities and institutions are using restorative and transformative justice methods. Here are some links if you would like to learn more about this alternative approach to justice.

Websites that teach restorative justice strategies for schools

- www.weareteachers.com/restorative-justice

- www.edutopia.org/blog/restorative-justice-resources-matt-davis

Resources on transformative justice

Beyond Survival: Strategies and Stories from the Transformative Justice Movement: www.akpress.org/beyond-survival.html

Transformative justice: https://transformharm.org

Addressing harm, accountability and healing: http://criticalresistance.org/resources/addressing-harm-accountability-and-healing

Podcast episode about Bear Clan Patrol: https://appointedpod.simplecast.com/episodes/ed761ba8-_YiNtUw_

Podcast episode featuring Mariame Kaba on moving past punishment: https://forthewild.world/listen/mariame-kaba-on-moving-past-punishment-151

Documentary profiling the Ojibway community of Hollow Water as they deal with an epidemic of sexual abuse in their midst: www.nfb.ca/film/hollow_water

Documentary that explores family violence and restorative justice from an Indigenous perspective: www.youtube.com/watch?v=lmstyXc6FnI

Participant Achievement Handout

Table A5.1: Participant achievement handout

CONGRATULATIONS!

You are now a Consent Culture creator!

Key points to remember:

- Consent is more than just "getting permission."
- Consent is a collaborative agreement about how we will play or share space together.
- Finding common ground is fun!
- Saying no is a skill that has to be learned.
- If you're a Maybe, say no.
- You can change your mind about what you are doing with your body, at any time, for any reason.
- Desire smuggling is normal, common, and a clue that you want something.
- The freeze response is one of the body's survival tactics. It's not a decision—it happens in an instant!
- Consent accidents happen, but the impact is what matters.
- Aim for repair and healing, not punishment.
- Take responsibility and apologize when you need to.
- Without consent, it's not sent.
- Be an upstander, not a bystander. Intervene when you see someone being targeted!
- An interaction is done when anyone in it wants it to be.
- You can create a warm, safe haven for one another and have fun.

To print out a more colorful "graduation certificate" version of this, or for a printable copy of the Power/Privilege Wheel, please visit www.creatingconsentculture.com/book-resources and use the password "book".

These are great to hand out at the end of the workshop. Optionally, you can add resources for local kids' helplines, or phone numbers for crisis lines on the other side of the certificate.

Participant Power/Privilege Wheel Handout

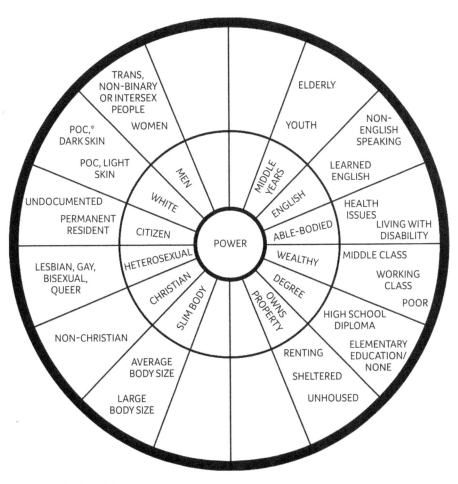

*POC: People of Color

Desire Smuggling Tactics

Table 10.1: Desire smuggling tactics

Mostly harmless, but not necessarily effective	May cause problems in a relationship and/or to self	Toxic and/or antisocial
• Hint about what you want • Find out if the other person wants the thing you want first • Talk about how "a lot of people do it" (instead of saying you want to do it) • Minimize it by saying "just" or "only" • Be loud and bombastic to distract from it • Want the other person to guess • Wait for the right time • Wait for a sign • Obsess about pros/cons • Overthink it • Send videos/links about the thing you want • Talk about it to everyone but the person/people who can give it	• Expect the other person to read your mind • Get drunk/high to remove inhibitions • Emotionally withdraw • Pester the other person to want it • Complain that you don't get it • Be "nice" and hope to be rewarded • Make unspoken deals • Give ultimatums • Tack on obligation to a "gift" • Guilt-trip • Be passive-aggressive • Blame them for not giving it to you • Hope and hope and hope • Settle for not getting it ever • Shame yourself for having that desire	• Bully • Belittle • Show contempt • Maliciously trick or deceive the other • Use emotional blackmail • Use actual blackmail • Threaten violence • Threaten suicide • Use force • Use violence • Steal • Assault

cont.

Mostly harmless, but not necessarily effective	May cause problems in a relationship and/or to self	Toxic and/or antisocial
• Tell a story/make art about the thing you desire • Post about it online • Play "options roulette" (where one option you give is the one you secretly want) • Offer to give the thing you want • Substitute something else • Avoid it altogether	• Shame others with the same desire • Spiritually bypass ("It's not good or holy to want that.") • Buy into a romance myth ("If you really loved me, you would do X") • Assume they should just *know* • Punish your partner for not giving it to you • Punish yourself/self-harm for wanting it • Make sugar-coated demands • Judge someone asking for what you want • Judge someone for getting what you want	

Additional Resources

BOOKS

Here is a short list of books that you may also be interested in. To see a growing list of books related to consent and consent education please visit the resources section of www.creatingconsentculture.com.

Talking Consent: 16 Workshops on Relationship and Sex Education for Schools and Other Youth Settings by Thalia Wallis and Pete Wallis

The Art of Receiving and Giving: The Wheel of Consent by Dr. Betty Martin with Robyn Dalzen

What Does Consent Really Mean? by Pete Wallis and Thalia Wallis

Consent on Campus: A Manifesto by Donna Freitas

Yes Means Yes: Visions of Female Sexual Power by Jaclyn Friedman and Jessica Valenti

Asking For It: The Alarming Rise of Rape Culture and What We Can Do About It by Kate Harding

Ask: Building Consent Culture: An Anthology edited by Kitty Stryker

Boys & Sex by Peggy Orenstein

Girls & Sex by Peggy Orenstein

The Hunting Ground by Kirby Dick and Amy Ziering

We Believe You by Annie E. Clark and Andrea L. Pino

The Body Keeps the Score by Bessel van der Kolk

Trauma-Proofing Your Kids: A Parents' Guide for Instilling Confidence, Joy and Resilience by Peter A. Levine and Maggie Kline

WEBSITES

Here are some related websites that you may find helpful. If you would like to see a growing list related to consent and consent education please visit the resources section of www.creatingconsentculture.com.

Hollaback! Training in the five Ds of bystander intervention: www.ihollaback.org

Speak About It Online programs that teach consent and sex education: https://wespeakaboutit.org

Scarleteen "Sex ed for the real world": http://scarleteen.com

Yes Means Yes Project Respect creates dialogue to create change in our communities: www.yesmeansyes.com

Teach Consent A short video and discussion guide: http://teachconsent.org

That's Not Cool Resources and connections for teens who want to change culture: https://thatsnotcool.com

Ask Roo An interactive bot that answers your questions about sex and relationships: https://www.plannedparenthood.org/learn/roo-sexual-health-chatbot

VIDEOS

Here are a few short videos that are great for kids young and old. For a growing list of great videos on consent, please visit the resources section of www.creatingconsentculture.com.

Let's Talk About Consent: www.youtube.com/watch?v=TBFCeGDVAdQ

Ask. Listen. Respect: www.youtube.com/watch?v=n6X5I7xoxEY

Get Consent, Ask, Listen: www.youtube.com/watch?v=zzuTjVwlcgo

Consent as Tea: www.youtube.com/watch?v=oQbei5JGiT8

Consent 101: www.youtube.com/watch?v=Ym2Gk4jD5Os

SAFETY RESOURCES

There are many online resources now that provide advice and assistance with the issues of consent that come up with online interactions. Here are a few that you may find helpful:

I Ask for Digital Consent—Tip Sheet: www.nsvrc.org/sites/default/files/publications/2019-01/Digital%20Consent%20Handout_508.pdf

Sexting laws by state across the USA: https://cyberbullying.org/sexting-laws

Canadian information about privacy, technology and sexting: www.cybertip.ca/app/en

A mobile app to help peers protect one another from sexual violence: www.circleof6app.com

Online safety plan for people experiencing harassment or abuse: https://breakthesilencedv.org/creating-a-digital-safety-plan

If you live with the person who is abusing you: www.scarleteen.com/safety_plan_when_you_live_with_the_abuse

CRISIS RESOURCES

Kids Help Phone 24-hour crisis line—A Canadian service for youth and young adults to access counseling services in French, English and Arabic: 1 800 668 6868; https://kidshelpphone.ca

RAINN online hotline based in the US: https://hotline.rainn.org/online (If you have been the victim of sexual assault, you can call the National Sexual Assault Hotline at 1 800 656 4673 or chat online at https://hotline.rainn.org/online)

Healthline—Sexual Assault Resource Guide based in the US: www.health-line.com/health/sexual-assault-resource-guide

Just the Workshop

To print Appendix 9, please go to creatingconsentculture.com/book-re-sources and use the password "book".

BEGINNING THE WORKSHOP

> Hello everyone, and thank you for being here. I have a vision of a future in which we as individuals and societies are kinder, more compassionate and more respectful to others and ourselves. This workshop is one tool to help move towards this vision and I thank you for joining me on this journey!

Take a few minutes and ask people to introduce themselves. Participants can give a name, state their pronouns, and say a little bit about what they hope to get from the workshop. You can also ask people to introduce themselves with one word that describes their current state of mind, or a fun fact about themselves, such as a favorite place, movie, or hobby.

> I would like to begin by acknowledging that we are holding this workshop on the traditional and unceded lands of the Sinixt Nation [for example].
>
> It's important for you all to know that I am required to report any disclosures of abuse. If anyone feels that they cannot stay in the room or needs assistance during the workshop, there is a support plan, and it is this...

If applicable, let the group know about your mandate to report. Please see Chapter 3 and Appendix 1 for more information.

> This is an interactive and experiential workshop, and we're going to be talking about consent, but mostly we are going to do exercises that help us practice what we are learning. If at any time you don't want to participate in an exercise, please feel free to sit on the sides and watch, but I encourage you to participate as much as possible, because the more you participate, the more you will get out of the workshop.
>
> Before we get started, let's make some group agreements about what is and isn't okay behavior in this group. Does anyone want to suggest an agreement that will make them feel safer during this workshop/exercise?

Write down ideas from the group. If the participants don't mention them, ask the group about adding the following:

- Respecting when someone is talking/no cross-talking.

- Having a designated space for sitting out if you're uncomfortable.

- No comments/observations from people while they are sitting out.

- Raising hands to speak.

> Alright, so can we all agree to these guidelines? Great, let's get started.
> Let's talk about consent. Does anyone here have a definition of what consent is?

Encourage a short discussion on what consent is. Be present, listen, and thank people for speaking. If people are hesitant to say anything, joke that it is not a test and there are no right or wrong answers, you're just curious to hear what ideas everyone has on the subject.

> Great! Thanks. In the past few years the popular concept of consent has evolved really quickly from "No means No" to "Get a verbal Yes" to "Anything but an enthusiastic Yes is a No." Another way to look at consent is as a collaboration, or "How are we going to play together?"

Many people think that consent is simple. One person asks for something and another person says yes or no. But the reality is that there is nothing simple about it. For starters, hopefully more than one person is asking for what they want! And it is likely that compromises are being made. There are a lot of factors that make creating consent between people more complicated. We'll talk about those factors as we go through the exercises.

When we are collaborating to make our interactions as mutually agreeable as possible, that is Consent Culture. We're going to talk more about collaboration and how to do it in a minute but first let's do some boundary exercises.

"No" exercises

Okay we're going to do a speaking exercise now. I'll be getting you to talk about touch, but no one is actually going to touch anyone.

I'm going to ask you to get into the pairs that we've formed, and remember who is an A and who is a B. A, your job is to ask B, "Would you give me a hug?" and B, your job is to say "No." Please say nothing else other than the word "No."

Even though you just instructed people to say only no, expect to hear all kinds of joking and making excuses. There will be laughter.

Great. Thank you. Now please trade places and do it again. So B, this time you will be asking for the hug, and A, you will say the word "No."

You'll probably have to give people about 30 seconds or so for each of these exercises in order to allow everyone a chance to get all the way through them.

Great. Thanks for doing that. How many people felt uncomfortable saying no?

As you ask these questions, raise a hand as encouragement to participants to also raise their hands if they agree.

How many people felt like making saying no into a joke? How many of you really wanted to explain to the other person why you were saying no even though we all just heard me tell you to say no?

People will be laughing and pointing at each other because they did just that.

Most people have a really hard time saying no. We don't want to let people down or disappoint them. We don't like conflict and we don't want to hurt people's feelings. Many people will do a LOT to avoid saying no, even when they really need to.

Let's try another exercise.

This time A will ask for a hug and B will say no. After B says no, I'd like A to say, "Thank you for taking care of yourself." Do that now please.

Once you feel they have all finished have them trade places and do it again.

Awesome. Thanks. Did it feel different saying no that time? What did you notice about how that changed the dynamic? How did it make you feel saying/hearing "Thank you for taking care of yourself"?

Allow for some discussion. Participants usually want to share what they are experiencing.

One of the ways that we create Consent Culture is by making sure our partner knows that we will hear and honor their No. When we actually thank our partner for honestly telling us that they are a No, we can help to undo a lifetime of learning that we are somehow being a bad person if we say no.

Before we go further into hearing and honoring No, I have to say, should you—or they—even be asking? Sometimes there are power differentials that make it almost impossible for people to say no, and in those cases even asking for touch is considered a form of harassment. If someone is your boss, supervisor, teacher, mentor, counselor, or just has a lot more power in the world than you do, they shouldn't even ask to touch you, or suggest that they would like it if you touch them. If there is a large power differential, it is the person with more power who must make sure that non-consensual or inappropriate actions don't happen.

Okay, on to consent in a situation where the people involved are on a relatively equal footing.

For the following demo, you can ask your assistant to join you, or use a broom or other prop.

Does this look like consent?

Lunge-hug either your assistant or a prop while simultaneously asking, "Hey want a hug?" so that you are already in full embrace before you finish asking the question. This should get some laughs.

Another way to create consent is to actually give your partner the time and space to be able to consider the request and give you an answer. If we ask and the person is silent that is also a No. Silence is a No. Hesitation is a No. Anything but an enthusiastic Yes is a No.

If you have an assistant you could do a demo here of a consensual hug with an ask and an enthusiastic Yes. You could also demonstrate thanking the assistant when they say no to a hug.

And by thanking the person for clearly stating their boundaries we can help them to feel more comfortable expressing themselves honestly. A person who has your best interests in mind will want to know what you truly want.

But what if someone says no to you and you are really struggling to accept their No? Maybe it really did hurt your feelings or you were super attached to how you imagined things going if they said yes. Please DO get help with working through your feelings and find someone to talk it out with. Your feelings are valid and it's good to talk about them. But please DO NOT expect the person who just said no to you to be that person. Having to hear about your upset feelings could feel like coercion to them, as if you're trying to guilt them into changing their answer.

But it's hard to say no!

We've all had the experience of having someone argue with us when we say no. But when it is about your choices around your body and touch, the attempts to argue with you or manipulate you may be quite sneaky. Here are some real-life examples of people NOT honoring or accepting a clear No.

If you have an assistant act this out with them, or use a prop. If you are a theatrical person, you can be more entertaining by giving a different character and voice to each of these statements.

What do you mean, "No"? What, you think you're all that?

You're so mean! You really hurt my feelings when you said no.

C'mon…just one kiss!

You're no fun! So cold.

Say the next statement with emphasis.

The more that someone argues against or does not accept your No, the more they are sending you red flags that they are not a safe person.

> And while we are on the subject, let's dispel the myth that most unsafe people will seem creepy or look threatening. The fact is that most serial predators are charming, charismatic people who are good at manipulating people into doing what they want. Otherwise, they would be a one-time predator, not a serial predator.
>
> Most attempts at manipulation are intended to put you in a position where you feel as if you have to defend your No, your character, or both. When it comes to your personal, physical autonomy, "No" is a complete sentence and you don't need to defend or justify your choice. You are allowed to walk away without saying anything more. You're not a bad person for saying no and disappointing someone. Life is full of disappointments and they will get over it.

Deliver this line for comedic effect.

> For example, I'm disappointed right now that [insert celebrity crush here] hasn't realized that we are soulmates, but I've learned to live with it.
>
> So, we're learning why it's important to make others feel comfortable to say no, and now let's look at why we should genuinely appreciate another person saying no to us.
>
> If we are the one asking, it can spare us a lot of confusion and self-doubt when people are clear about their boundaries. No is important information for everyone involved. Please get into your pairs again and pick an A and a B. A, your job is to ask for a hug, and B, your job is to say no to the hug, but without using the words, "no" or "not", or shaking your head.

You may have to go over these instructions a couple of times. People often need to double check what they're not allowed to say or do.

> Okay great. Let's trade places and do it again please.

It will probably take 30 seconds to a minute for each person to have a chance to play both roles. There is usually laughter.

> Thanks for doing that. How did that feel? When you were asking for the hug, did you wish that the other person could just say no?

Encourage discussion on the take-aways from this exercise as time allows.

For those of you who struggle to say no, remember how good it feels to get a clear answer. Having the ability to give a clear authentic No means that your Yes is more meaningful and heartfelt.

Also if you have a hard time saying no, remember that every time you say no to one thing you are saying yes to another. No to a party could be Yes to a movie with a good friend. No to spending time with a friend could be Yes to more time learning an instrument. In fact, every No contains an infinity of possible Yes's.

Many cultures value personal sacrifice for the good of the family or the community over all else. Other cultures value individualism. When your family or community wants something from you, it can be hard to say no. Saying no may be harder or easier for you to begin with, but most of us can use more practice.

I'd like everyone to get up and walk around the room please. When you find yourself in front of someone, pair off and take turns asking for a hug and saying no. This time I want you to respond graciously to hearing no and use different wording. You could say things like, "Thank you for being clear," or, "Thanks for knowing your boundaries." Find a way to thank people that feels right for you.

Thanks for doing that. On to the next section!

What if I'm a Maybe?

I used to be the kind of person who always said maybe instead of no just to avoid the discomfort of saying no to someone. Then I would go home and stress out about still having to either say no or do the thing that I didn't want to do. I would live under a cloud of anticipation until finally resolving the situation at the last minute.

Now if I'm not sure whether I'm a Yes or No, I default to No and give myself the space and time to figure out what I really want. If I go home and decide I was actually a Yes I can always change my mind. It's easier to change a No to a Yes than to change a Yes to a No, although either is fine. Being free to change your mind as your situation changes means you're listening to your inner wisdom.

But what if you've thought about it and you still really can't tell if you are a Yes or a No? And sometimes you need to know right away. There might be a couple of reasons for this.

One reason is that there are at least three different kinds of enthusiastic Yes's:
- The first is that you really want something.
- The second is that you aren't sure if you want it, but you are excited to try it and find out if you like it.
- The third is that someone else wants it and you are wholeheartedly willing to give it to them. Like a gift.

This last type of Yes is different from tolerating, enduring or going along with something. If it feels that you are tolerating something happening to you, that's a No.

The second reason you might not know if you are a Yes or a No is something I call the Habitual Yes. That's when we find ourselves saying yes before we've even had a chance to think about the question, as if it were unthinkable that we might say anything else. When saying yes has become a habit, it takes practice to change, just like breaking any bad habit.

Being aware of why you're saying yes will help you to have clearer boundaries with something. If it feels that you are tolerating something happening to you, that's a No.

Next are two different exercises to help the participants to feel into their bodies, their Yes and their No. You can choose one, or do both. The first one involves the participants getting up and moving around the room, while the second has them sitting still.

Option 1: Active

We're going to try a quick exercise in feeling into your body when you are feeling Yes and when you are feeling No. I'd like everyone to get up and walk around the room looking for objects that make you feel like saying Yes. Objects only, and not other people or anything that they're wearing or carrying. When you find one, look at that object and notice how you feel in your body. Say Yes to the object.

After a couple of minutes have them do the same thing with an object that is a No for them.

Now please walk around until you find an object that makes you feel No. Say no to the object. Look at it for a bit and notice how your body feels.

Option 2: Seated

I'm going to take you on a little guided meditation now. Please sit up straight, and if it helps you to visualize, close your eyes. Take a deep breath into your belly. Breathe in through your nose and breathe out through your mouth. With your next deep breath feel your face and neck relax [long pause]. As you breathe deeply feel your shoulders and back relax [long pause]. Feel your breath going down into your belly as your arms and hands loosen [long pause]. As you take another deep breath feel your legs relax and your feet sink into the floor [long pause]. As you sit comfortably with your muscles in a relaxed position, notice how your body feels. As I guide you to explore different feelings, keep noticing your body. Do your shoulders hunch up? Does your belly tighten? Does it become harder to breathe? Easier?

Continue to breathe deeply and think about something that makes you angry or upset.

[Pause] How does your body feel now?

[Pause] Now think about something that makes you happy or excited.

[Pause] How does your body feel now?

Open your eyes now. Could you feel the difference in your body between the positive and the negative statements? If so, what did it feel like?

Other possible questions are:

- "What do you think about saying no when you're not sure about something?"
- "Did you feel Yes and No in different parts of your body?"
- "How do you feel when you ask someone to do something, and they say maybe?"
- "Any other 'aha!' moments to share?"
- "Did anyone fall asleep?"

Changing your mind

> I want to stress how important it is to know that you always have the right to change your mind during personal interactions. You are NOT signing a contract when you decide to spend time with someone, kiss them, touch them, or any other activity. Even if you are in a relationship and living with someone, or even married to them, you still have the right to have changing boundaries, from moment to moment. Just because you wanted to do something yesterday, or five minutes or even five seconds ago, does not mean that you should want to do it again right now.

In the next bit, Erica talks about how her personal boundaries have changed with a demonstration that usually helps people visualize their boundaries and how they can change. You will have to find a way to describe this boundary strategy that suits you.

> The reality is that we often don't know exactly where a boundary is until right after it is crossed. I used to be the kind of person who trusted people too much, too quickly and I kept my boundaries close like this, so that when they were crossed I would be hurt.

Hold your arms in front of you in a semicircle with your hands close to your chest and then use one hand to show how crossing that line immediately impacts your chest.

> Over time I have learned to keep my boundaries further out, so that when they are crossed I am still okay.

Move the semicircle further out from your body, so that this time when you use one hand to demonstrate crossing that line it is far enough from your chest that it doesn't make contact.

> Depending on how well I know the person, or how safe I feel, I can move my boundaries further out, or closer in.

Use your semicircle of arms to demonstrate moving a midway boundary closer in, then further out. For a laugh, you can orient yourself towards someone and in a joking way put your arms out as far as possible with an exaggerated look on your face. Only do this if you're confident you can pull it off in a way that is funny and doesn't hurt anyone's feelings.

This business of feeling into your body, and noticing what it feels like to say or do the opposite of what you actually want, takes practice, so we're going to lead on to another exercise that helps participants do that in a fun way. You'll be splitting them into groups of three, but if the numbers are wrong, one or two groups of four will still work. If you do have a group of four, let them know that their individual turns will be a little shorter.

> Okay, we're going to do a fun exercise to practice what we've just learned. For this exercise, we're going to split up into groups of three. Once you're in your group of three I want the group to pick someone to be the first No person.

Once everyone is divided up and the No people have been chosen, continue on.

> Okay, No person, your job is to say no to everything. No matter how much you want to say yes, you have to say no. The other two people in the group, your job is to ask the No person things that make it hard to say no. An example could be, "Can I give you some money?" or, "Would you let me do your chores for you?" No asking about anything to do with sex or violence please. If you are the No person, remember to check in with how your body is feeling when you say no to something you would rather say yes to. Okay, you can start now please.

After a minute or so get them to switch to another No person. If you have groups of four, approach that group a little sooner and get them to switch. After another minute or so repeat the process so that everyone in each group gets a turn as the No person. There is usually a lot of laughter during this exercise.

Great. Thanks for doing that. We're going to do that again except this time the No person is a Yes person. This time it is your job to say yes to everything. You're not going to DO anything, but you have to say yes. The other two, your job is to ask questions that make it hard for the Yes person to say yes. An example could be, "Will you listen to some poetry I just made up?" or, "Could I have your cell phone please?" Again, no questions about sex or violence. If you are the Yes person, remember to check in with how your body is feeling when you have to say yes to something you would rather say no to.

Once again get them to change Yes people every minute or so, until everyone has had a turn. Encourage a discussion of what they got out of the last exercise. Some possible questions are:

— "How did it feel to say no when you wanted to say yes?"
— "How did it feel to say yes when you wanted to say no?"
— "Did you notice any sensations in your body?"
— "Any 'aha!' moments to share?"

Consent is collaboration

Alright, so we've practiced saying no and yes and knowing which one we are. We've practiced hearing no and appreciating clarity, and learned about how it's okay to change your mind. Now let's talk about collaboration.

Depending on how well I know the person, or how safe I feel, I can move my boundaries further out, or closer in.

But first, I'm going to ask you all to think of a tree. If you like, you can close your eyes and try to really see it.

Give them a moment to do this.

Can anybody tell me what kind of tree they thought of? What did you imagine when you thought of a tree? How about you?

Get a sampling of tree visions from the group.

Now, if we are all thinking of such different things when we hear the word "tree," how much more complicated would the differences be if we were talking about words like "love" or "relationship" or "society," or almost any word at all? I'd like you to keep that in mind as we do the next exercise.

We're going to get up and move around and do some greeting exercises now. This can look like shaking hands, fist bumping, hugging, bowing, or waving. Or another kind of greeting of your own creation. If you are too uncomfortable with an exercise or any part of it, just sit it out.

Please get up and walk around the room. Look at the other people walking around the room.

Let them walk around for a minute.

Now let's all end up standing in front of someone.

Pause until everyone has a partner. If it's an odd number either you or your assistant can be a partner while you are leading, or ask three people to be a group.

Without saying any words, use your facial expressions and body language to collaborate with your partner to have the most mutually agreeable greeting.

Give them a minute or so until everyone has had a chance to figure out how they will greet each other. There will probably be some laughter but if you hear people talking remind them that you've asked them to do this without speaking.

Thank you. Now, silently to yourselves, think about what you liked, and what you didn't like about that style of greeting.

Great. Let's walk around the room and look down at other people's feet.

Give them a minute or so to walk around.

> Stop when you find yourself in front of a friendly pair of feet. We're going to greet each other again, except that this time we won't make eye contact or look for body language. We'll keep looking at our feet, and rely entirely on our verbal communication to collaborate to have the most mutually agreeable greeting possible.

Give them a couple of minutes for their greetings. People will be relieved to be able to speak again, but also many will be feeling uncomfortable about not making eye contact, so there will likely be some awkward laughing and a fair bit of talking.

> Great, thank you. Now think about what you liked, and didn't like, about that style of greeting.
> All right, let's walk around the room some more and this time you can look at people's faces again.

Give them a minute to walk around looking at each other again.

> Stop when you find yourself in front of someone that you haven't greeted yet. This time we will use all of the skills from the first and second greetings. So, facial expressions, body language, and verbal communication are all used to collaborate on the most mutually agreeable greeting possible.

Give them a couple of minutes to make sure that everyone has a chance to figure out their greeting.

> And now think about what you liked and didn't like about that style of greeting.

At this point you can let everyone sit down again.

> Which kind of greeting was your favorite?

Give a minute for responses. Participants may be trying to argue why one of the greeting exercises was better than the others.

> There is no right or wrong answer to this. Some people even prefer the one where we stare at our feet. Everyone has different communication styles and it's good to know which ones you prefer to use when you're trying to collaborate with someone for a positive interaction. The way others communicate may not be the same way you do, and this can lead to misunderstandings.
>
> Another question: When you were checking in with your greeting partner, how many of you asked the question "Is this okay?" We want to reach for a higher standard than "Okay". If your partner is saying, "Okay" or, "I don't mind" or, "I guess" or, "Sure," that's not enthusiastic consent. A good way to avoid miscommunication is to seek enthusiastic consent, and ask questions that have to be answered with full sentences, such as, "What would you like to do?" or, "Tell me what would make you happy."

Encourage discussion on this topic of how miscommunication can happen or has happened to people. Some questions that could be helpful for this include:

> – "What did you notice about yourself during these greeting exercises?"
> – "Which was your favorite style of greeting and why?" (Participants are often amazed to learn that not everyone has chosen the same favorite greeting exercise.)
> – "What else besides different communication styles can cause misunderstandings?"
> – "What are some things we can do to avoid miscommunication?"

Asking for what you want

> We've gone over how most people have a hard time saying no, and now we're going to talk about the asking. The truth is, most people also have a hard time asking for what they want.
>
> We have a lot of different reasons for not asking for what we want. Maybe we are scared of feeling vulnerable, or fear being rejected. Maybe we don't want to make others feel pressured. Maybe we are so sure that we can't receive what we want, that we see no point in asking. Maybe we don't spend much time thinking about what we truly want.

But if consent is collaboration, and only one person is asking for what they want, then that is a very limited collaboration. If neither of them is asking for what they want, it's a guessing game! To have an effective collaboration we each need to be comfortable asking for what we want, as well as being comfortable to say no or yes.

Often when we feel uncomfortable to ask for what we want, we do something called "desire smuggling," where we try to get what we want without having to ask. This can range from dropping hints to complex manipulative maneuvers all the way to extremely violent and antisocial behavior. Desire smuggling is natural and common, but it becomes toxic when we're not prepared to honor another person's No.

But a lot of us don't allow ourselves to even think about what we really want. Discovering what we want and learning how to ask for it takes practice.

I'm going to ask you to get into your pairs again, and remember who is A and B, and face each other. A, your job is to ask B, "What do you want?" B, you're going to come up with something you want. It can be ridiculous or totally unrealistic, but it cannot involve sex or violence. Once B says the thing they want, A responds with, "Thanks for letting me know."

Ask for as many things as you can think of for 30 seconds, and I'll tell you when to stop. Go!

Great. Now A and B trade places, so that B is asking, and do that again. Ask for as many things as you can for the next 30 seconds, and Go!

Even if you are already good at asking for what you want, you can play this game with friends to help them get more comfortable with it as well. If you struggle with asking for what you want, you can practice with a friend, until it comes more easily.

Sometimes we ask for something we think we want, and then once we get it we realize we don't really want it. Even if you were the one to ask, you are still allowed to change your mind. And just because you can't figure out exactly what you want at first, it's okay to keep asking until you figure it out.

Here are some possible questions for unpacking the exercise:

- "How did it feel to be asked about what you want?"
- "How did it feel to be thanked for sharing it?"
- "How did it feel to thank someone else for sharing what they want?"
- "Any 'aha!' moments that anyone would like to share?"

Like a deer in the headlights

There is one more thing we need to talk about in order to explain the importance of enthusiastic consent…

Has everyone here heard of the "flight or fight response"?

Give people a chance to respond. If someone brings up the freeze response, congratulate them for guessing what you were about to talk about.

We now know that there is a third response, the freeze response, that is even more common than the other two responses. Does anyone here know anything about the freeze response?

Allow a short discussion here.

The freeze response is also known as tonic immobility and it is a result of the body going into survival mode, but seeing no chance of success with fight or flight. For animals in nature it is called "playing dead" and it is the body trying its best to keep itself safe. This is an unconscious reaction made in milliseconds, not a decision. It just happens. And it happens faster than this!

You can snap your fingers to demonstrate.

People who experience this feel immobilized and disconnected from their bodies. Often, they cannot speak coherently, or even speak at all. During this response, they have trouble forming memories.

People who experience the freeze response can feel confused and ashamed because they don't understand why they were unable to fight or run away. They don't understand that their body had a reaction that was out of their control.

You can help people who've experienced the freeze response by talking about it, recognizing it when you see and hear about it, and not judging people for having this uncontrollable response. If someone tells you about having been unable to speak, or run, or fight, or having fuzzy memories, and not understanding why, you can tell them, "You did what you needed to do to survive." And then you can tell them about the freeze response and how it was not their fault.

Enthusiastic consent exercises

Unfortunately, because many of us don't understand that this is a natural response to a traumatic event, people may judge themselves or be judged by others. People who are unaware may misinterpret silence and a lack of movement as passive consent. Remember, only ENTHUSIASTIC consent is consent. If you are unsure, ask for and receive an enthusiastic Yes before you do anything. You can have fun with that. Let's do that now.

Can everyone give me their version of an extremely enthusiastic Yes? I'll show you mine.

Do your most theatrical and entertaining version of an enthusiastic Yes. Have fun with it!

Okay, now everyone else.

Get everyone to enthusiastically say yes at the same time.

Substitution for older groups

For older groups, you may want to discuss the connection between the freeze response and sexual assault. You could tell them this:

When there is a perceived threat to your survival, you will instinctively have one of three responses: fight, flight or freeze. This happens within 15 milliseconds of perceiving the threat. It's an autonomic response common to all mammals, and it is completely outside a person's conscious control. The amygdala sends signals to the hypothalamus, which releases hormones telling the autonomic nervous system to change your heart rate, breathing, vision, and hearing, and it even thickens your blood and redistributes your blood flow. Activity in your prefrontal cortex diminishes, as well as in other parts of your brain, which messes up your ability to form memories of the event. All this happens before a full second goes by.

Studies show that the freeze response is the most common response to sexual assault, and that once people have experienced the freeze response one time, they are more likely to experience it during future events.

When children are abused by adults they usually have a freeze response, since fighting back or fleeing will often not be options for them. And as these children grow into adults, the freeze response may become their default response. They are also more likely to develop PTSD.

> This is why in intimate partner situations it's especially important to get enthusiastic consent. Someone experiencing a freeze response will be unable to give enthusiastic consent, even if they can mumble or murmur.

As the facilitator, you can include the enthusiastic Yes exercise above and/or follow up with some discussion questions that are more mature, such as:

> - "How do you know when someone is unenthusiastic with their Yes?"
> - "What are some ways you might be able to tell if someone is in a freeze response?"
> - "How can you support someone who is blaming themselves for not fighting back?"

Backup, not backlash

> Let's talk about when we mess up, because none of us is perfect, and we all make mistakes and hurt other people, even when we don't mean to. In Consent Culture, when someone is hurt, we focus on supporting the person in pain, and prioritize what they need to feel supported. The person who did the hurting is expected to be accountable and make amends. This can feel scary at first, because maybe you've taken responsibility for something before and then been punished. But that's not how we do things in Consent Culture.
>
> Has anyone heard of restorative justice?

Give a moment for answers.

> Right now, we have a punitive justice system, but many Indigenous peoples have traditionally used a system of restorative justice, and it's having a resurgence of popularity now. It's called restorative justice because rather than focusing on punishing wrongdoing, it focuses on restoring harmony to a community.
>
> In a restorative justice system, everyone in the community engages by standing up to bad behavior, supporting people who've been targeted, and encouraging those who have harmed others to apologize and make amends.
>
> Let's talk about an example. If one of you was to film yourself calling a classmate names until they cried, and then shared that video online, what do you think would normally happen?

Get some answers. Keep asking questions until you get the full picture of what would happen to the student who did the harassing, the student who was harassed, and how it might impact both students' family members or classmates. For instance, if the harasser were suspended, would the victim feel safer when they returned to school?

> Now, if we were in this restorative system that meets the needs of the person harmed and strives to restore harmony to everyone involved, what do you think would happen?

Again, keep asking questions and gently guide the conversation until the participants can get a general picture of the harassed student being supported, the student who did the harassing taking accountability, the root causes of the action being explored, and everyone coming out of it feeling better understood and that it won't happen again.

You could ask questions like:

> – "What do you think the difference is between accountability and punishment?"
> – "How can we back up the person who has been harmed?"
> – "How can we support the person who did the harm to take accountability?"
> – "What actions or words would help you feel more confident that this wouldn't happen again?"

> Let's talk about harassment. We all know what it's like to be a bystander when someone is being harassed or bullied, and many of us know the pain of being targeted while people stand by and watch. Let's not stand by, let's stand up when we see someone targeting someone else. In Consent Culture, we are upstanders, not bystanders.
>
> What do you think some examples of being an upstander might look like?

You can get a few examples and perhaps add a few yourself, such as:

•   Getting help when someone is being harassed.

•   Intervening if you feel safe to.

- Trying to distract the person who is doing the harassing so that the person being targeted can get away.

In Consent Culture, we want to be good at apologizing when we've hurt someone. By being good at it, I don't mean putting on a good show. Let's learn what is involved in apologizing well and practice it.

I'm going to apologize to the group now, and I want you to grade me. I'm really sorry if something I did made you feel bad.

How was that? Do you feel like my apology was sincere?

Get some feedback from the group before you try again.

Okay, how's this? I'm really sorry that I made you do some weird exercises. I know that it made you feel embarrassed, and I didn't want to make you feel that way.

How was that? Was it better when I was more specific about what I did wrong and how it made you feel? How could we make it better?

Okay, one last try. I'm really sorry that I made you do some weird exercises. I know that it made you feel embarrassed, and I don't want you to feel that way. I'm going to try really hard not to make you do any more weird exercises.

How was that? Was it better that I said how I was going to change my behavior so that I wouldn't do it again?

Just to be clear, that was all for practice, and I am going to have you do more weird exercises!

− "Any 'aha!' moments from this demonstration?"
− "Will you apologize differently after this? Why, or why not?"

Taking it online

Creating Consent Culture is something we can do online as well as in real life. Let's look at the tools we've already learned, and how they apply to our online interactions.

Practicing saying and hearing no, thanking others for expressing clear boundaries, and checking in with ourselves to know what we want and don't want are important skills for interacting online.

Defaulting to a No when we are a Maybe, being clear communicators, and being an upstander rather than a bystander are all great ways to contribute to a better culture online.

Let's do a quick brainstorm. Let's break into our groups of three and take a minute to talk about some of the challenges of communicating online. See if you can come up with a few ways that online interactions can be hard. Please get into your groups and do that now.

After a minute or two, stop the discussion and ask the group for a few examples that they've come up with.

Clearly some things are different online, and there are a few extra tools that can help us with those added challenges. One thing that happens online is that people feel removed from the interaction and are likely to show less empathy. People tend to say things online that they wouldn't say in person and conflicts can arise and escalate quickly. Sometimes there are misunderstandings because we can't hear the person's tone of voice or see their body language.

Those are some of the challenges, but one of the benefits of online interactions is that we can step away from our devices and check in with ourselves. Then we can either decide not to take part anymore, or else come back when we are calm and clear about what we need to say.

We've all said things online that we regret, and if we can keep in mind that it is harder to take things back once they are out there on the internet, perhaps we can make better choices about what we share.

The next time you have an interaction online that is upsetting you, try taking a break and using the embodied check-in before going back to the conversation. Maybe you'll decide you don't want to go back to that conversation at all!

I'm going to show you a tool that's called, "Why am I sharing this?" Let's pull out a sheet of paper and put together a checklist of things to think about before you share or post.

They can include, "Is this a kind thing to say?", "Is this helpful?" or, "Is this really true?."

Does anyone want to share any of their pre-posting conditions?

Give a moment for discussion.

When you have a list of considerations that you like, you could put a little sticker on your phone to remind yourself to go over that checklist before hitting "post" or "send". Maybe you want to challenge yourself to do this every time for a couple of weeks and see if you can turn it into a habit.

We can also be upstanders rather than bystanders online, and intervene when we see someone being targeted. For example, we can respond publicly in a thread. We can take people aside privately or in their direct messages and talk about how they are hurting someone. And, most importantly, we can check in with and support those being targeted.

What other ideas do you have for how to be an upstander online?

Give a moment for discussion.

Let's keep in mind that being online has been shown to decrease our ability to be empathetic, so we need extra time to step back and make sure we're bringing the same amount of empathy and compassion to our virtual encounters as we do in person. That's a challenge for everyone!

Finally, why not pause before we give advice online, and ask ourselves, "Did they ask for advice?" We might think that we have the perfect words of wisdom, because we've been through that experience before. One way to bring Consent Culture to the internet is to ask, "Do you want advice, someone to listen to you, or something else?" Or ask if there is a way that you can help.

If you are given advice that you didn't ask for, and it's upsetting, take a deep breath and remind people that you would like to be asked if you want advice before it is offered.

When is the hug over?

This brings us to our final question: When is the hug over? Consent is a thing given from moment to moment and in Consent Culture you are encouraged to change your mind at any time. When a handshake, a hug or any physical interaction is consensual, it should end when one person decides they are done. We usually rely on body language to understand when this is, but that's not always clear, and some people are better at reading body language than others.

Let's find a partner and pick an A and a B for one last greeting. Actually, two greetings. This works best with either a handshake or a hug, so if that doesn't appeal to you just sit it out.

Decide together if you're going to do a handshake or a hug for this exercise. Then, shake hands or hug your partner and A, you will be the one to stop first. B, try to get as close as you can to noticing exactly when A decides to stop. Once you've done that, trade places and do it again. Really try to see if you can pinpoint the exact moment the other person wants to stop.

If someone is not picking up on your cues, use your words. You can say, "Thank you, I'm done now." Or, "That was nice, let's stop now."

Does anyone have any "aha!" moments or anything that they would like to share from this greeting exercise?

We are nearing the end of the workshop now, and I'd like us to practice a few of the skills we've learned so far. I'm going to ask you to walk around the room and ask for handshakes, or hugs, or fist bumps, or high fives, or a wave, and this time if you are a Yes you can say yes and do those things. But you have to say no at least every other time. In other words, if you said yes this time, say no the next time, even if you would like to say yes.

You can also spend the whole exercise practicing your No. Remember to thank your partners when they say no.

Let this go on for a few minutes. Play it by ear.

Thanks everyone. We've practiced saying and hearing yes and no and how to check in with ourselves to know whether we are a Yes or a No. We've talked about changing our minds and checking in with our partners. We've learned different ways to collaborate for a mutually agreeable interaction and practiced knowing when the interaction is over.

Practice, practice, practice

Learning Consent Culture and unlearning all the stuff that makes it harder takes practice. You may not get this right the first time, or the second time, or the twentieth time, and that's okay. Keep practicing and it will become clearer each time. You will get better at it. You may have times when you think, "I could have done that better" or, "I wish I had listened more closely" or, "I should have kicked their ass!" but please don't be hard on yourself. This does not come automatically to anyone and we all need to practice. If you don't know how to be kind to yourself, close your eyes and think of someone that you love very much. Now, imagine treating yourself the same way you would treat them.

Another thing to remember is that sometimes there are situations where it is not safe to say no or state your boundaries no matter how much you want to. That is not the time to practice! If you find yourself in a situation like that, trust your instincts, and do and say whatever it takes to stay safe and extract yourself from that dangerous situation. Ask for help from someone you trust afterwards.

> We are coming to the end of the workshop and we will have time for questions and a discussion. You can see me afterwards if you have questions. Now there is just one more demonstration.

At this point if you don't have an assistant, ask if one of the participants is willing to come up and violate your boundaries for the demonstration. This usually gets a laugh.

> Okay, you know how to have consensual interactions now, but what about when you go out in the world and run into people who don't? I'm going to demonstrate a few ways to handle people crossing your boundaries.

If you do have an assistant, ask them to come up and when they are standing beside you ask them to violate your boundaries. You could ask them to touch your arm or hug you without asking, if you are both comfortable with that.

The first time they violate your boundaries, pull back and say, "Oh, I need to be asked for touch."

The second time, move their hand away or step back and say, "Not cool."

The third time, pull away and say, "I didn't hear you ask me if I wanted to do that—have you heard of Consent Culture?"

Thank your assistant/participant for helping in the demonstration. Turn to the group.

> Congratulations everyone! You've completed the workshop and you are now certified Consent Culture creators. Thank you for helping to create Consent Culture.

Hand out certificates of completion if you have them. If you have time, take questions and mediate a discussion of "aha!" moments from the workshop.

Possible questions:

> - "Does anyone have any 'aha!' moments from the workshop that they would like to share?"
> - "What do you feel is the most important thing you learned over the last few hours?"
> - "What is one thing you will do differently after taking this workshop?"

Glossary

#METOO movement: A social movement started by Tarana Burke in 2006 advocating for survivors of sexual harassment or violence to speak out about their experiences in order to center and support them.

Assault: The act of inflicting physical harm or unwanted physical contact on a person or, in some specific legal definitions, a threat or attempt to commit such an action.

Autonomy/bodily autonomy: An individual's right to make decisions regarding their own body, including deciding at any point who may or may not touch their body in any way. Also referred to as bodily sovereignty.

Boundaries: Guidelines, rules, or limits that a person creates to identify reasonable, safe, and permissible ways for other people to behave towards them and how they will respond when someone passes those limits.

Canceling: A modern form of ostracism in which someone is thrust out of social or professional circles—whether it be online, on social media, or in person—as a consequence of something they have said or done. Those who are subject to this ostracism are said to have been "canceled." This can be a traumatic form of bullying among young people.

Coercion: The intimidation of a victim to compel the individual to do some act against their will by the use of psychological pressure, physical force, or threats.

Coercion culture: A society or an environment in which conformity, compliance, and authority are valued over an individual's needs, desires, or integrity.

Conscious bias: The attitudes and beliefs we have about a person or group on a conscious level. This includes being aware of personal prejudice in favor of or against one thing, person, or group compared with another, usually in a way that is considered to be unfair. An individual, group, or institution may hold conscious biases, which are also known as explicit biases.

Consent: An agreement about how two or more people are going to interact or share space together. These agreements are clear, informed, voluntary, sober, act- and person-specific, ongoing, mutual, active, and come directly from the individuals engaging in the activities.

Consent accident: A somewhat controversial term used to denote a consent incident that was not intentional. Determining intent is relevant to repairing harm. However, "accident" should not be used to minimize or downplay the impact on the person harmed.

Consent culture: A society or environment in which creating explicit agreements, looking for common ground and respecting boundaries is the norm, for both sexual contact and everyday activities.

Consent incident: Any occurrence where consent was violated, or was fuzzy or unclear. While it is used somewhat interchangeably with "consent violation," this term is meant to be more neutral in its assumption of intent, and includes incidents across the range of intentional, unskillful, and accidental. Impact is still the most important consideration in creating repair.

Consent violation: A transgression or infringement on a stated agreement, or proceeding to take action on another person in the absence of consent.

Desire smuggling: Hiding what you really want from yourself and/or a loved one, while finding covert strategies to get (at least pieces of) what you want. These covert strategies range from the innocuous to the destructive, and occur as a means to avoid vulnerability and shame.

Digital consent: Permission given for texting, sharing online information or images.

Digital footprint: A trail of data you create while using the internet. This includes the websites you visit, emails you send, postings and information you submit to online services like social media, shopping, game and dating apps.

Dominant culture: Includes the lifestyles, customs, manners, and morals that override others within a particular political, social, or economic entity, in which multiple cultures are present.

Empty consent: Occurs when a person says or signals yes to something, but is psychologically disassociated, or coerced or manipulated into doing so.

Facilitation: The art of making experiences more accessible to your participants than they would be without you. To make something easier, to bring about.

Fawn response: A learned trauma response in which a person reverts to people-pleasing to diffuse conflict and re-establish a sense of safety.

Freeze response: Also known as "tonic immobility," this is an autonomic response to extreme stress or perceived danger. As with the fight and flight responses, it is an instantaneous reaction of the amygdala, not the conscious mind.

Gender: May refer to both gender roles and gender identities. The social and cultural role of each sex within a given society is one part of gender. People often develop their gender roles in response to their environment, including family interactions, the media, peers, and education. There is also a spectrum of gender identities that can change over time and vary widely within and across cultures. Western culture tends to conceive of gender as binary. However, many other cultures have three or more genders. In contrast, the term sex is used to indicate the biological differences between male, female, and intersex people.

Gender inequality: The social process by which people are treated differently and disadvantageously, under similar circumstances, on the basis of *gender*.

Habitual Yes: A pattern of, or compulsion towards, agreeing to requests without pausing to consider the impact or implications on one's time, energy, or resources.

Harassment: Unwelcome or offensive behavior by one person to another that can be sexual or non-sexual in nature. Examples include making unwanted sexual comments or jokes to another person, sending unwanted sexual texts, bullying, or intimidation.

Inclusive: Activities, curricula, language, and other practices in the educational environment that attempt to ensure every student's access to and participation in learning.

Modeling: A general process in which individuals serve as examples to others, exhibiting the behavior to be imitated by others. These examples are internalized without comment or discussion.

Parentified: Parentification is the process of role reversal whereby a child is obliged to act as parent to their own parent or sibling. In extreme cases, the child is used to fill the void of the alienating parent's emotional life.

Permission: The right or ability to do something that is given by someone who has the power to decide if it will be allowed. Implies gatekeeping, authority, and/or a power differential. While permission is a part of consent, consent is not permission. One *gets* permission. Together, we *create* consent.

Power dynamics: The way different people or different groups of people interact with each other. It may refer to how one person leverages their power over another, or to the interplay of different expressions of and bids for power among people.

Privilege: A special right, advantage, or immunity granted or available only to a particular person or group. This may be formalized via rules, laws, or policy, or be informal as a custom or social norm.

Racialized: Racialization or ethnicization is a political process of ascribing ethnic or racial identities to a relationship, social practice, or group that did not identify itself as such. To categorize, marginalize, or regard according to race.

Rape: A type of sexual assault that involves vaginal, anal, or oral penetration using a body part or an object without consent. Rape is a form of sexual assault, but not all sexual assault is rape.

Rape culture: A society or environment whose prevailing social attitudes have the effect of normalizing or trivializing sexual assault and abuse.

Relational intelligence: The sum of learned skills that enables us to navigate relationships well.

Restorative justice: An approach focused on repairing harm when wrongdoing or injustice occurs in a community. Restorative justice centers support for the victim, and involves the offender, their social networks, justice agencies, and the community.

Revenge porn: The sharing of sexually explicit images or video without consent, and as a means of retaliation. These images or videos may be made with or without the knowledge of the victim.

Sexting: Sending, receiving, or forwarding sexually explicit messages, photographs, or images. Consensual sexting may still create a legal problem for people who are under age.

Sexual abuse: Any sort of unwanted sexual contact, including but not limited to, force, threats, or taking advantage of an individual, often over a period of time. A single act of sexual abuse is usually referred to as a "sexual assault."

Sexual assault: Any unwanted sex act committed by a person or people against another person. Examples include, but are not limited to, non-consensual kissing, groping, or fondling; attempted rape; forcing someone to perform a sexual act; and rape. Specific definitions of sexual assault vary from state to state and from country to country.

Sexual harassment: Any unwanted comment, gesture, or action that is sexual in nature that makes someone feel afraid, embarrassed, uncomfortable, or ashamed.

The intention of the person doing the action doesn't matter, it's the negative impact the action has that makes something sexual harassment.

Sexual violence: An umbrella term that refers to any form of non-consensual sexual behavior, including sexual assault, sexual abuse, sexual harassment, sexual exploitation, sex trafficking, and sexual violence facilitated through technology.

Sharenting: The practice of parents posting content about their children on internet platforms. The term covers pitfalls resulting from the spectrum of typical family sharing all the way to parents being exploitative and manipulative.

Socialization: The process of internalizing norms and ideologies of the societies in which we grow up or participate. Socialization involves both conscious and unconscious learning and teaching and is a means for social and cultural continuity. Socialization is a part of developmental psychology.

Social justice: The view that all people deserve to enjoy the same economic, political, and social rights and opportunities, regardless of race, sex, gender, gender identity, socioeconomic status, sexual identity, ability, or any other characteristics.

Transformative justice: A series of practices and philosophies designed to create change in social systems. Mostly, they are alternatives to criminal justice in cases of interpersonal violence, or are used for dealing with socioeconomic issues in societies transitioning away from conflict or repression. At its most basic, transformative justice seeks to respond to violence without creating more violence or by engaging in harm reduction to lessen the violence.

Trauma-informed: An approach to teaching and facilitation that acknowledges the effects of individual and systemic trauma on participants, and considers how instruction and participation can be adjusted in order to ensure a safer and more supportive learning environment.

Unconscious bias: Social stereotypes about certain groups of people that individuals form outside their own conscious awareness. Studies show that we all hold unconscious beliefs about various social and identity groups, stemming from the tendency to organize social worlds by categorizing, in accordance with cultural and historical context. Unconscious bias is also known as implicit bias.

Upstander: A person who speaks or acts in support of an individual or cause, particularly someone who intervenes on behalf of a person being attacked or bullied.

Victim blaming: A ubiquitous attitude in the current culture of coercion. Victims of a crime or any wrongful act are held partially or entirely at fault for the harm that was done to them.

Acknowledgements

ERICA

There are so many people who have helped me on the winding road to this book and throughout its development. First and foremost, I'd like to thank Marcia for being the best co-author a person could hope for, and for starting Cuddle Party in the first place and working so hard to create an organization that was there for me when I needed it.

I would like to bow deeply to all the consent and sex educators of the past (and present!) who paved the path for us to be able to get to this point, and I'd especially like to thank my friends Grace Caligtan and Danyale Thomas for patiently and gently giving me much-needed feedback as I began to facilitate the Consent Culture Intro workshop.

I also want to thank my very supportive kids, nieces, and nephews who generously let me try out the first (and very clumsy!) version of the workshop with them, and for taking the time to offer up helpful feedback as well. It was very sweet of them to mock me only lightly.

My heartfelt thanks to Mandira Srivastava for inviting and generously hosting me in Delhi, India, where she kindly supported me on this journey of bringing Consent Culture to the world, one workshop at a time. Much gratitude to the Rex Karmaveer Global Fellowship for recognizing this consent education work with an award for social innovation. So many people made me feel welcome in India, and I look forward to visiting again someday!

A very big shout out to my Honolulu WomanSpeak group led by Dany-ale Thomas! The support and encouragement of all of these beautiful and talented women helped me to find my voice and my confidence. It was on the very first "girl trip" of my life with this fantastic group of women that I had the inspiration to turn the workshop into a book.

Once I had a rough draft, I felt very lucky to have my most esteemed writer and consent educator friends Rose Nielson, Jasmine Joy Love, Shawn Coleman, and Grace Caligtan read through it and give me many important points to think about, bringing more clarity to the book.

Finally, much gratitude to Emily Badger of Jessica Kingsley Publishers for believing in what we are doing, and for making the publishing process so easy.

This workshop and this book have truly been a collaborative effort, and I hope to continue to collaborate with Consent Culture creators the world over for many years to come.

MARCIA

There are so many people who have cleared the way for this book to come to fruition, but none more so than my Cuddle Party colleagues: Reid Mihalko, who co-created Cuddle Party with me all those many years ago; Len Daley, who held the vision; Madelon Guinazzo, Adam Paulman, and Soleiman Bolour, who steer the ship today. I'm grateful to every Cuddle Party facilitator and participant worldwide who has shared their experiences, feedback, and critiques with me—I've learned from you all.

I am endlessly grateful to my dear friend and colleague, Betty Martin, whose insights and nuances about human interactions have shaped both this book and my life in countless ways. Without your work with Cuddle Party and the Wheel of Consent, and your unwavering support, this book would not have been possible.

Erica, you kept me on track and managed my chaos to make this book a reality. Thank you for your patience with me as we birthed this baby. There are not enough words to express my gratitude to you for bringing this project to me.

Carmen Leilani, Katie Spataro, and Shauna Farabaugh, every conversation with each of you reminds me of why this work is important. Kathryn Toohey and Stephanie Saline, you are my anchors and without you, I would have drifted far out to sea.

My heartfelt thanks to M'kali-Hashiki Nin and Julie Lythcott-Haims, who provided invaluable feedback on the manuscript and made this book better in every way.

A huge shout out to William Winters, Ruby Rogers, Misha Bonaventura, Elle Beigh, Jason James, and all the other sex-positive organizers, performers, teachers, community builders and producers in the Bay Area and beyond, who are committed to building Consent Culture through their events and who consistently do the hard work of being human together.

Finally, my undying gratitude to Alethea Power, who has believed in me since day one, to Nelz Carpentier, without whose material support this book could not have happened, and to JB for keeping me in memes, snacks and hoodies. And especially to Mark Everett—your patience and love has steadied me more than you will ever know. I love you all from the bottom of my heart.

About the Authors

Marcia Baczynski has been writing, teaching and coaching about sexual communication and consent for over 20 years. In 2004, she co-created Cuddle Party, a workshop and social event about boundaries, communication, and touch. In her private practice, she works with clients to discover what they want and how to talk about it (even if it's off the beaten path). Marcia lives in the San Francisco Bay Area. You can find her online at www.askingforwhatyouwant.com.

Erica Scott is the creator of The Consent Culture Intro Workshop and the concept for this book. As a survivor of child sexual abuse, 20-plus years of working in a male-dominated industry, and as a mother of young adult children, she feels the urgency to bring more effective consent education to a wider audience. In 2019, she was awarded the Rex Karmaveer global award for social innovation. You can find out more about Erica at www. creatingconsentculture.com.

Endnotes

HOW TO USE THIS BOOK

1   Appiah, K.K. (2020). The Case for Capitalizing the B in Black. *The Atlantic*. https://www.theatlantic.com/ideas/archive/2020/06/time-to-capitalize-blackand-white/613159.

Laws, M. (2020). Why we capitalize "Black" (and not "white"). *Columbia Journalism Review*. https://www.cjr.org/analysis/capital-b-black-styleguide.php.

CHAPTER 2

2   Folchert, K.E. (2008). *Institutional Perpetuation of Rape Culture: A Case Study of the University of Colorado Football Rape and Recruiting Scandal*. UCLA: Center for the Study of Women. https://escholarship.org/uc/item/2n56g086.

Pazzanese, C. (2020, August 25). How rape culture shapes whether a survivor is believed. *The Harvard Gazette*. Retrieved from https://news.harvard.edu/gazette/story/2020/08/how-rape-culture-shapes-whether-a-survivor-is-believed.

Sexual Harassment & Rape Prevention Program (SHARPP). University of New Hampshire. Retrieved from www.unh.edu/sharpp/rape-culture.

3   Essien, E.D. (2018). Ethical audit of prosperity gospel: Psychological manipulation or social ministry. *International Journal of Knowledge-Based Organizations*, 8(2), 53–66. doi: 10.4018/978-1-7998-2457-2.ch009.

Kinmond, K. & Oakley, L. (2015). Working Safely with Spiritual Abuse. In Dr P.M. Gubi (ed.) *Spiritual Accompaniment & Counselling* (pp. 145–162). London: Jessica Kingsley Publishers.

4   Catholic Church child sexual abuse scandal (2019, February 26). BBC News, www.bbc.com/news/world-44209971.

Wu, K.J. (2019, May 27). Study finds misconduct spreads among police officers like contagion. Nova Next, www.pbs.org/wgbh/nova/article/police-misconduct-peer-effects.

Thorbecke C. & Ghebremedhin, S. (2018, March 16). Alaska Airlines pilot accuses co-pilot of rape in lawsuit, calls it a "not-dealt-with issue in our industry." ABC News, https://abcnews.go.com/GMA/News/alaska-airlines-pilot-accuses-pilot-rape-lawsuit-calls/story?id=53785721.

5   Cable, C. (2017). I Sing of Misogyny and Sexual Assault: Rape Culture in Contemporary American Pop Music Contemporary American Pop. Honors thesis. University of Iowa, https://ir.uiowa.edu/cgi/viewcontent.cgi?article=1070&context=honors_theses.

Lynskey, D. (2013, November 13). Blurred Lines: The most controversial song of the decade. The Guardian International Edition, www.theguardian.com/music/2013/nov/13/blurred-lines-most-controversial-song-decade.

6   Dodgson, L. (2017, November 12). A lot of problematic behaviour from male characters in films is supposed to be romantic—here's why it isn't. Business Insider, www.businessinsider.com/this-behaviour-in-romantic-films-is-problematic-2017-11.

Grady, C. (2018, September 27). The rape culture of the 1980s, explained by Sixteen Candles, Vox, www.vox.com/culture/2018/9/27/17906644/sixteen-candles-rape-culture-1980s-brett-kavanaugh.

7   McNamarah, C.T. (2019). White caller crime: Racialized police communication and existing while Black. *Michigan Journal of Race and Law*, 24(2), 335–416. https://repository.law.umich.edu/mjrl/vol24/iss2/5.

Weaver, V.M. (2018, May 29). Why white people keep calling the cops on black Americans. Vox, www.vox.com/first-person/2018/5/17/17362100/starbucks-racial-profiling-yale-airbnb-911.

8   Ross, J. (2014, March 26). The creepy way fathers across the country are controlling their daughters' virginity. Mic, www.mic.com/articles/86149/the-creepy-way-fathers-across-the-country-are-controlling-their-daughters-virginity.

Hesse, M. (2019, November 7). Why do so many dads think it's their duty to monitor their daughters' virginity? The Washington Post, www.washingtonpost.com/lifestyle/style/why-do-so-many-dads-think-its-their-duty-to-monitor-their-daughters-virginity/2019/11/07/be8ffaee-016c-11ea-9518-1e76abc088b6_story.html.

9   Gender, Equality and Diversity and ILOAIDS Branch (2019, June). Violence and harassment against persons with disabilities in the world of work. Conditions of Work and Equality Department International Labour Office, www.ilo.org/wcmsp5/groups/public/---dgreports/---gender/documents/briefingnote/wcms_738118.pdf.

Equality and Human Rights Commission Great Britain (2014). Studies on Disability-Related Harassment. Health and Human Rights Resource Guide, www.hhrguide.org/2014/03/24/example-1-studies-on-disability-related-harassment.

10 Employment and Social Development Canada (2020, June 24). Government of Canada publishes new regulations to prevent harassment and violence in federal workplaces. Newswire, www.newswire.ca/news-releases/government-of-canada-publishes-new-regulations-to-prevent-harassment-and-violence-in-federal-workplaces-801575510.html.

Boesch, D., Frye, J., & Holmes, K. (2019, January 15). Driving Change in States to Combat Sexual Harassment. Center for American Progress, www.americanprogress.org/issues/women/reports/2019/01/15/465100/driving-change-states-combat-sexual-harassment.

11 Berger, M.W. (2020, October 23). How have new social norms emerged as COVID-19 has spread? Penn Today, https://penntoday.upenn.edu/news/Penn-philosopher-Cristina-Bicchieri-studies-social-norms-COVID.

Bavel, J.J.V., Baicker, K., Boggio, P.S. *et al.* (2020). Using social and behavioural science to support COVID-19 pandemic response. *Nature Human Behaviour*, 4, 460–471. https://doi.org/10.1038/s41562-020-0884-z.

12 Brockes, E. (2018, January 15). #MeToo founder Tarana Burke: "You have to use your privilege to serve other people." The Guardian, www.theguardian.com/world/2018/jan/15/me-too-founder-tarana-burke-women-sexual-assault.

Gill, G. & Rahman-Jones, I. (2020, July 9), Me Too founder Tarana Burke: Movement is not over. Newsbeat BBC, www.bbc.com/news/newsbeat-53269751.

13 Chenoweth, E. & Pressman, J. (2017, February 7). This is what we learned by counting the women's marches. The Washington Post, www.washingtonpost.com/news/monkey-cage/wp/2017/02/07/this-is-what-we-learned-by-counting-the-womens-marches.

Broomfield, M. (2017, January 23). Women's March against Donald Trump is the largest day of protests in US history, say political scientists. Independent, www.independent.co.uk/news/world/americas/womens-march-anti-donald-trump-womens-rights-largest-protest-demonstration-us-history-political-scientists-a7541081.html.

14 Tippett, E. (2019). Non-disclosure agreements and the #MeToo Movement: What do we do now? American Bar Association Dispute Resolution Magazine, www.americanbar.org/groups/dispute_resolution/publications/dispute_resolution_magazine/2019/winter-2019-me-too/non-disclosure-agreements-and-the-metoo-movement.

Levy, K.M. (2019, May 21). Breaking the silence: Good riddance to non-disclosure agreements in the #MeToo Era. Rutgers University Journal of Law & Public Policy, https://rutgerspolicyjournal.org/breaking-silence-good-riddance-non-disclosure-agreements-metoo-era.

15 Garber, M. (2018, January 2). Is this the next step for the #MeToo Movement? The Atlantic, www.theatlantic.com/entertainment/archive/2018/01/beyond-metoo-can-times-up-effect-real-change/549482.

Brown, J. (2019, September 17). Men sound off on #MeToo: "I definitely look back and cringe." NBC Better By Today, www.nbcnews.com/better/lifestyle/men-sound-metoo-i-definitely-look-back-cringe-ncna1054886.

16 Naide, S. (2020, January 15). State lawmakers say yes to consent education. Guttmacher Institute, www.guttmacher.org/article/2020/01/state-lawmakers-say-yes-consent-education.

Landman, K. (2019, August 8). How #MeToo is changing sex ed policies, even in red states. NBC News, www.nbcnews.com/health/kids-health/how-metoo-changing-sex-ed-policies-even-red-states-n1039616.

17 Thomlinson, R. (2020, May 14). Bill C-65 and the prevention of harassment and violence. Lexology, www.lexology.com/library/detail.aspx?g=e618d732-4906-4e8b-a8f8-8024ae0dd704.

Sullivan, N. (18 Nov, 2019). Cape Breton, provincial schools teach rules of consent, healthy relationships. Saltwire, www.saltwire.com/atlantic-canada/news/canada/cape-breton-provincial-schools-teach-rules-of-consent-healthy-relationships-377580.

18 Khan, U.A. (2019, November 16). Impact of "METOO" movement on implementation of POSH Law. Pleaders, https://blog.ipleaders.in/metoo-movement-implementation-posh-law.

Marathe, H. (2020, October 14). "No #MeToo for women like us": Poor enforcement of India's Sexual Harassment Law. Human Rights Watch, www.hrw.org/report/2020/10/14/no-metoo-women-us/poor-enforcement-indias-sexual-harassment-law.

19 Maier, S.L. (2008). "I Have Heard Horrible Stories..." Rape victim advocates' perceptions of the revictimization of rape victims by the police and medical system. *Journal of Violence Against Women*, 14(7), 786–808. www.ojp.gov/ncjrs/virtual-library/abstracts/i-have-heard-horrible-stories-rape-victim-advocates-perceptions.

Walklate, S. & Clay-Warner, J. (2017). Victimization and Revictimization. In T. Sanders (ed.) *The Oxford Handbook of Sex Offences and Sex Offenders* (pp.270–286). Oxford: Oxford University Press, https://psycnet.apa.org/record/2016-47934-013.

20 London Police Service (2019). Review of "Unfounded" Sexual Assault Cases. London Police Reports and Statistics, www.londonpolice.ca/en/about/review-of--unfounded--sexual-assault-cases.aspx.

Johnson, H. (2020, February 3). Rape myths and sexism still cloud police responses to sexualized violence. Policy Options, https://policyoptions.irpp.org/magazines/february-2020/rape-myths-and-sexism-still-cloud-police-responses-to-sexualized-violence.

21 Decker, E.M. (2017, November 27). No rape kit should go untested amid #MeToo movement. The Hill, https://thehill.com/opinion/criminal-justice/361988-no-rape-kit-should-go-untested-amid-metoo-movement.

Bowen, A. (2020, April 16), She woke up naked and bloody. 8 months later, she still awaits her evidence. Why Illinois' rape kit backlog still hasn't been fixed. Chicago Tribune, www.chicagotribune.com/lifestyles/ct-life-illinois-rape-kit-tracking-system-backlog-20200416-paegm7uokzaxxpskb3tz2ldj5m-story.html.

22 Huston, C.M. (2015). Restorative Justice: A Comparative Analysis of Campus Implementation. Honors thesis. Honors College, University of Maine, https://digitalcommons.library.umaine.edu/honors/218.

Blas Pedreal, M.L. (2014). Restorative Justice Programs in Higher Education. *The Vermont Connection*, 35(5). https://scholarworks.uvm.edu/tvc/vol35/iss1/5.

CHAPTER 3

23 Levin, S.T. (2019, June 21). "This is all stolen land": Native Americans want more than California's apology. The Guardian, www.theguardian.com/us-news/2019/jun/20/california-native-americans-governor-apology-reparations.

Grandin, G. (2020, January 20). Slavery, and American racism, were born in genocide. The Nation, www.thenation.com/article/society/slavery-american-genocide-racism.

24 Sallquist, P. (2020, August 10). Land acknowledgement—What is it and why is it important? UCDS Institute, www.ucds.org/land-acknowledgement-what-is-it-and-why-is-it-important.

Keefe, T.E. (2019). Land acknowledgement: A trend in higher education and non-profit organizations. www.researchgate.net/publication/330505687_Land_Acknowledgement_A_Trend_in_Higher_Education_and_Nonprofit_Organizations.

25 Joseph, B. (2019) *Guidebook to Indigenous Protocol*. Indigenous Corporate Training, www.ictinc.ca/guidebook-to-indigenous-protocol.

26 Collier, L. (2016, November). Growth after trauma. American Psychological Association, www.apa.org/monitor/2016/11/growth-trauma.

Kaufman, S.B. (2020, April 20). Post-traumatic growth: Finding meaning and creativity in adversity. Scientific American, https://blogs.scientificamerican.com/beautiful-minds/post-traumatic-growth-finding-meaning-and-creativity-in-adversity.

27 Minahan, J. (2019, October). Trauma-informed teaching strategies. *Educational Leadership*, 77(2), 30–35. www.ascd.org/publications/educational_leadership/oct19/vol77/num02/Trauma-Informed_Teaching_Strategies.aspx.

Knight, C. (2014, February 19). Trauma-informed social work practice: Practice considerations and challenges. *Clinical Social Work Journal*, 43(1), 25–37. doi: 10.1007/s10615-014-0481-6.

28 Wolfe, D.S. (2012, April). Revisiting child abuse reporting laws. *Social Work Today*, 12(2), 14. www.socialworktoday.com/archive/031912p14.shtml.

Mathews, B. & Kenny, M. (2008). Mandatory reporting legislation in the United States, Canada, and Australia: A cross-jurisdictional review of key features, differences, and issues. *Child Maltreatment*, 13(1), 50–63. www.researchgate.net/publication/5676349_Mandatory_Reporting_Legislation_in_the_United_States_Canada_and_Australia_A_Cross-Jurisdictional_Review_of_Key_Features_Differences_and_Issues/citation/download.

CHAPTER 5

29 Martin, B. & Dalzen, R. (2021). *The Art of Receiving and Giving: The Wheel of Consent*. Eugene, OR: Luminaire Press. https://wheelofconsentbook.com.

30 Channel 4 (2017, February 2). These Kids Do NOT Like This Lemonade. *The Secret Life Of 5 Year Olds*. www.youtube.com/watch?v=KD9-jnLD4lY.

CHAPTER 8

31 WBTV (2017, June 23). Women can't revoke consent to sex once underway, NC law states. www.wbtv.com/story/35735579/women-cant-revoke-consent-to-sex-once-underway-nc-law-states.

Burns, J. (2017, September 15). In North Carolina, women can't legally revoke consent after sex begins. Forbes, www.forbes.com/sites/janetwburns/2017/09/15/under-north-carolina-law-women-cant-revoke-consent-after-sex-begins/?sh=6b7b6bfa5c84.

32 McGinn, D. (2019, November 18). Mothers have "boys don't cry" bias, new study suggests. The Globe and Mail, www.theglobeandmail.com/canada/article-mothers-have-boys-dont-cry-bias-new-study-suggests.

Mayer, D.M. (2018, October 8). How men get penalized for straying from masculine norms. Harvard Business Review, https://hbr.org/2018/10/how-men-get-penalized-for-straying-from-masculine-norms.

33 1in6 (n.d.). The 1 in 6 Statistic, https://1in6.org/get-information/the-1-in-6-statistic.

34 Stemple, L. & Meyer, I.H. (2014). The sexual victimization of men in America: new data challenge old assumptions. *American Journal of Public Health*, 104(6), e19–e26. doi: 10.2105/AJPH.2014.301946.

Vitelli, R. (2020, April 1). Why aren't male victims of sexual abuse speaking out? Psychology Today, www.psychologytoday.com/ca/blog/media-spotlight/202004/why-arent-male-victims-sexual-abuse-speaking-out.

35 Government of Western Australia Department of Health (n.d.). Common myths about sexual assault, https://healthywa.wa.gov.au/Articles/A_E/Common-myths-about-sexual-assault.

The University of Tennessee Knoxville (n.d.). For Male Survivors of Sexual Assault, Counseling Center, https://counselingcenter.utk.edu/self-help-materials/for-male-survivors-of-sexual-assault.

CHAPTER 11

36 MacDermott, D. (2018, May 8). Why women freeze during sexual assault. Psychology Today, www.psychologytoday.com/ca/blog/modern-trauma/201805/why-women-freeze-during-sexual-assault#_=_.

37 Ending Violence Association of BC (n.d.). The "freeze" response to sexual violence. BC Association of Clinical Counselors, https://bc-counsellors.org/freeze-response-sexual-violence.

Windegger, T. (2018, June 29). What's with the freeze response? www.youtube.com/watch?v=zAVU3tlKC0c.

CHAPTER 12

38 Ordway, D.-M. (2018, October 5). Why many sexual assault survivors may not come forward for years. The Journalist's Resource, https://journalistsresource.org/health/sexual-assault-report-why-research.

39 Lorenz, K., Kirkner, A., & Ullman, S.E. (2019). A qualitative study of sexual assault survivors' post-assault legal system experiences. *Journal of Trauma Dissociation*, 20(3), 263–287. doi: 10.1080/15299732.2019.1592643.

Chemaly, S. (2016, August 16). How police still fail rape victims. Rolling Stone, www.rollingstone.com/culture/culture-features/how-police-still-fail-rape-victims-97782.

40 Adams, L. (2018, March 1). Sex attack victims usually know attacker, says new study. BBC News Scotland, www.bbc.com/news/uk-scotland-43128350.

National Institute of Justice (2008, September 30). Most victims know their attacker. https://nij.ojp.gov/topics/articles/most-victims-know-their-attacker.

41 The Canadian Press (2015, May 1). Rehtaeh Parsons documentary looks at final years of torment. CTV News, www.ctvnews.ca/canada/rehtaeh-parsons-documentary-looks-at-final-years-of-torment-1.2354402.

Hart, C.G. (2019, May 28). How reporting sexual harassment impacts a woman's career. Fast Company, www.fastcompany.com/90355363/how-reporting-sexual-harassment-impacts-a-womans-career.

42 Marsh, C. (2019, November 1). Honoring the global Indigenous roots of restorative justice: Potential restorative approaches for child welfare. Center for the Study of Social Policy, https://cssp.org/2019/11/honoring-the-global-indigenous-roots-of-restorative-justice.

Zellerer, E. (1999, September 1). Restorative justice in Indigenous communities: Critical issues in confronting violence against women. *International Review of Victimology*, 6(4), https://journals.sagepub.com/doi/abs/10.1177/026975809900600406?journalCode=irva.

43 Goodstein, J. & Butterfield, K.D. (2010, July). Extending the horizon of business ethics: Restorative justice and the aftermath of unethical behavior. *Business Ethics Quarterly*, 20(3), 453–480. www.jstor.org/stable/25702409?seq=1.

We Are Teachers Staff (2019, January 15). What teachers need to know about restorative justice. We Are Teachers, www.weareteachers.com/restorative-justice.

44 Morin, A. (2020, February 24). How psychology explains the bystander effect. Very Well Mind, www.verywellmind.com/the-bystander-effect-2795899.

Brewster, M. & Tucker, J.M. (2016). Understanding bystander behavior: The influence of and interaction between bystander characteristics and situational factors. *Victims & Offenders*, 11(3), 455–481. doi: 10.1080/15564886.2015.1009593.

45 www.ihollaback.org.

CHAPTER 13

46 Green, E. (2019, February 15). How technology is harming our ability to feel empathy. Street Roots, www.streetroots.org/news/2019/02/15/how-technology-harming-our-ability-feel-empathy.

Pfeil, U. & Zaphiris, P. (2007). Patterns of empathy in online communication. Conference on Human Factors in Computing Systems—Proceedings. 919–928. www.researchgate.net/publication/221514615_Patterns_of_empathy_in_online_communication.

47 https://knowyourmeme.com/memes/sharenting.

48 Baron, J. (2018, December 16). Posting about your kids online could damage their futures. Forbes, www.forbes.com/sites/jessicabaron/2018/12/16/parents-who-post-about-their-kids-online-could-be-damaging-their-futures/?sh=7d9b-6f2627b7.

Pringle, R. (2018, November 28). Parents are giving tons of their kids' personal data away—and the long-term effects aren't yet known. CBC News, www.cbc.ca/news/technology/kids-digital-footprint-personal-data-1.4826929.

49 Kavenna, J. (2019, October 4). Shoshana Zuboff: "Surveillance capitalism is an assault on human autonomy." The Guardian, www.theguardian.com/books/2019/oct/04/shoshana-zuboff-surveillance-capitalism-assault-human-automomy-digital-privacy.

Saha, D. (2020, May 20). How the world became data-driven, and what's next. Forbes, www.forbes.com/sites/googlecloud/2020/05/20/how-the-world-became-data-driven-and-whats-next/?sh=1348028957fc.

50 Day, R. (2019, July 29). How revenge porn has been driving victims to suicide attempts. Manchester Evening News, www.manchestereveningnews.co.uk/news/greater-manchester-news/how-revenge-porn-been-driving-16635743.

Winiecki, E. (2013, May 22). Cyber bullying of rape victims: Modern day version of stoning. Girl's Globe, www.girlsglobe.org/2013/05/22/cyber-bullying-of-rape-victims-modern-day-version-of-stoning.

Index

What Does Consent Really Mean?

Pete Wallis and Thalia Wallis

Illustrated by Joseph Wilkins

£15.99 | $23.95 | HB | 64PP |
ISBN 978 1 84819 330 7 |
eISBN 978 0 85701 285 2

"Consent is not the absence of 'NO', it is an enthusiastic YES!!"

While seemingly straightforward, Tia and Bryony hadn't considered this subject too seriously until it comes up in conversation with their friends and they realize just how important it is.

Following the sexual assault of a classmate, a group of teenage girls find themselves discussing the term consent, what it actually means for them in their current relationships, and how they act and make decisions with peer influence. Joined by their male friends who offer another perspective, this rich graphic novel uncovers the need for more informed conversations with young people around consent and healthy relationships. Accompanying the graphics are sexual health resources for students and teachers, which make this a perfect tool for broaching the subject with teens.

Pete Wallis is a senior practitioner in Restorative Justice for Oxfordshire Youth Justice Service UK and a founding member of the charity SAFE! Support for young people affected by crime.

Thalia Wallis is a relational psychotherapist who supports young victims of crime, as well as delivering psycho-educational workshops in schools to increase students' mental well-being and resilience.

Joseph Wilkins is a freelance illustrator and designer based in Oxford. He graduated from Falmouth College of Arts in 2006. His website can be found at www.josephwilkins.co.uk.

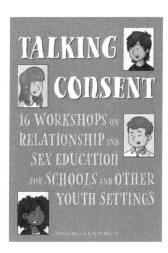

Talking Consent

16 Workshops on Relationship and Sex Education for Schools and Other Youth Settings

Thalia Wallis and Pete Wallis

£26.99 | $39.95 | PB | 304PP |
ISBN 978 1 78775 081 4 |
eISBN 978 1 78775 082 1

This book provides teachers and parents with the 'need-to-knows' to educate groups of young people about consent, pornography, sexting, and many other related topics, as well as giving them the tools to ward themselves against abusive behavior.

Initiating a discussion with young people on topics around sex can seem daunting, but Talking Consent *is full of lesson plans, workshops*, and creative ideas for introducing and promoting constructive discussions around these areas—while also dispelling common myths, and giving appropriate answers to difficult questions that may arise from these discussions.

Inclusive of everybody, including the LGBT+ community and people with disabilities, this book will provide professionals with the information they need to spark and shape conversation around these complex issues in an assured way.

Pete Wallis is a senior practitioner working in youth justice, and a founding member of the charity SAFE! Support for young people affected by crime, which works across the Thames Valley. Pete has written and co-written several books on restorative justice and related topics for JKP and Policy Press.

Thalia Wallis is a relational psychotherapist with over ten years' experience supporting distressed, vulnerable, and traumatized young people in various settings including education and criminal justice. Thalia is co-author of *What Does Consent Really Mean?*, a graphic novel for teenagers published by JKP.

Let's Talk Relationships

Activities for Exploring Love, Sex, Friendship and Family with Young People

Vanessa Rogers

£24.99 | $32.95 | PB | 160PP | ISBN 978 1 84905 136 1 | eISBN 978 0 85700 340 9

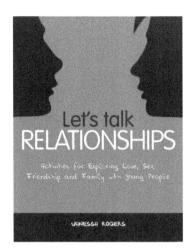

Let's Talk Relationships offers a multitude of creative ways to get young people aged 13–19 talking about positive relationships, helping them to stay safe, healthy, and happy. Ideal for groups or one-to-one work, this resource features over 90 tried-and-tested activities.

Focusing on peer friendships, personal relationships, and family dynamics, issues covered include peer pressure, relationship bullying, decision-making, managing conflict at home, and family values. Activities come complete with photocopiable worksheets and include ideas for storyboard work, games, role-play, and quizzes, as well as suggestions for creative projects including drama, music, and art activities. They are designed to build assertiveness skills, encourage young people to make positive choices, and help them to talk about their feelings. This second edition is fully updated and contains over ten new activities in each of the five sections.

This is an invaluable resource for all those working with young people, including youth workers, teachers, and voluntary sector youth leaders, helping them to make sessions valuable, educational, and enjoyable.

Vanessa Rogers is a qualified teacher and renowned youth worker with over ten years' experience both at practitioner and management levels. Prior to becoming a nationally acclaimed youth work consultant, Vanessa managed a wide range of services for young people including a large youth centre and targeted detached projects in Hertfordshire, UK. Vanessa's website can be found at www.vanessarogers.co.uk.

Horny and Hormonal

Young People, Sex and the Anxieties of Sexuality

Nick Luxmoore

£18.99 | $26.95 | PB | 224PP |
ISBN 978 1 78592 031 8 |
eISBN 978 1 78450 278 2

Ellis's mother is angry because he's been watching porn. Sheron says she hates her body. Mitchell is upset because Jack doesn't want to have sex with him…

Sex affects everything. It may not be the single most important thing in a young person's life, but it's always important and a crucial means by which young people try to understand themselves, whether they're in sexual relationships, on the brink of sexual relationships or watching from afar. Yet sex and sexuality are subjects that many adults (including parents, counselors, teachers and other professionals) are wary of talking about with young people.

This book is about helping young people feel less anxious about sex and sexuality. It's also about helping professionals feel more confident. Weaving case material with theory and discussion, Nick Luxmoore describes vividly the dilemmas faced by so many young people and suggests ways of supporting them effectively at such a crucial and sensitive time in their lives.

Nick Luxmoore was a school counselor, trainer, teacher, youth worker, and UKCP-registered Psychodrama psychotherapist. He had over 35 years' experience of work with young people and with the professionals who support them. He worked as the counselor at King Alfred's Academy in Wantage, UK.